The Literature of Food

ALIMENTUM

ISSUE ONE   WINTER   2006

PUBLISHER/EDITOR
Paulette Licitra

EDITOR
Peter Selgin

POETRY EDITOR
Cortney Davis

DESIGN
Claudia Carlson
Peter Selgin

PUBLICITY DESIGNER
Tim Maxwell

WEB DESIGNER
Leigh Wood

EDITORIAL ASSISTANT
Diana Pittet

SPECIAL THANKS TO
Cynthia Brown
Abigail Kirsch, Inc.
Marion Neidkowski
James Racheff, Jr.
Robert Rabinowitz

ALIMENTUM SPONSOR
The French Culinary Institute,
New York City

ALIMENTUM ADVISORY BOARD
Mark Kurlansky
Micol Negrin
Bonnie Slotnick
Polly Talbot
Clifford A. Wright

Alimentum is published
twice yearly Winter & Summer

SUBSCRIPTIONS
$18 per year
Please add $5 for Canadian
and foreign subscriptions.
Single copies $10.

Make checks payable to

ALIMENTUM
P.O. Box 776,
New York, NY 10163

DISTRIBUTED BY
Ubiquity Distributors and
Bernhard DeBoer, Inc.

SUBMISSIONS
Manuscripts are read year round.
Please see website for details.

www.alimentumjournal.com

EMAIL INQUIRES TO
editor@alimentumjournal.com

© 2005 BY ALIMENTUM.
ALL RIGHTS RESERVED.

ISBN # 0-9773528-0-3

Contents

PUBLISHER'S PREFACE / 5

FICTION

Beef—David Plumb / 7
Onigiri—Lisa Beatman / 10
The Absence of Everything Else—Douglas W. Milliken / 22
Sweet Potatoes—Elizabeth Anne Socolow / 27
Bon Appetit—Peter Gray / 40
Rolling Boil—Janna McMahan / 42
Pancakes—Alexa Raine-Wright / 53
The Soup—Mark Kurlansky / 63
She Likes My Hair—Evan Morgan Williams / 80

POETRY

Grocery Store Diva: Three Poems—Carly Sachs / 14
Chinese Restaurant Suite: Three Poems—Richard Berlin / 24
Almond and Chocolate—Cortney Davis / 36
Stew—Ann Pelletier / 48
Three Poems—Gaylord Brewer / 49
Italian Cuisine—Paul Hostovsky / 75
Chutney—Elizabeth Weir / 92
Two Poems—Robert Faguet / 103
Three Poems—Leslie McGrath / 106
Why I Write—Esther Cohen / 120

NONFICTION

Memoir of a Utensil Meal—Mina Samuels / 18
Watching Him Cook—Meredith Escudier / 33
Hawaiian Tooth—Oliver Sacks / 38

In the Soup—Andrew Daubigny / 68
Ode to Risotto—Donald Newlove / 77
Scurvy—Lanard W. Polis / 94
Tomorrow's Butter—Gerald Busby / 99
Eating with the Dogon—Clifford A. Wright / 109
The Schumanwich—Rebecca Schuman / 118

INTERVIEW
Mark Kurlansky / 56

COVER ART & ILLUSTRATIONS
Peter Selgin

Publisher's Preface

J.D. Salinger's character, Seymour Glass, advises his fiction-writing brother, Buddy, to imagine what he'd most want to read and then to sit down, shamelessly, and write the thing himself. I've taken that good advice one step further. I'm publishing what I'd most like to read.

Because I love literature and I love food, when I read about food I want more than a recipe list, more than a restaurant critique, more than a description of exotic cuisines sampled in faraway places. I know that food has a personal presence in our lives—it's not just a matter of taste and culture. Food also simmers in our hearts—like music, nature, and dreams. We all know it; we all feel it. But who's writing about it? As it turns out, a lot of people. Their stories, poems and essays are what make *Alimentum*.

My guess is I'm not the only one who's thrilled, tickled, and awed by the exciting material this first issue of *Alimentum* has elicited and inspired. What follows in these pages is what I'd most like to read.

And I'm betting that you will, too.

Paulette Licitra

When I get a little money, I buy books. And if there is any left over, I buy food.
   —Desiderius Erasmus

Beef
by David Plumb

I told you about the downsizing. I call it out-sizing. I should have seen it coming. The not enough days off, or too many days off. Or because I know, for real, that my job may be on the line with the Pisces FR-9000 high speed fish filleter, that can measure the length of a fish, adjust for the value of the fish, cut and figure out the ratio of bone size to fish size. Who can keep up? Or the TRIO Top Skinner that whips through three hundred fillets per minute. Guaranteed against split tails and ragged edges. They call it a smart machine. This makes me feel crazy. I wonder what they call me?

So, I end up in jail for meat. Not fish. Hamburger. I don't even eat meat unless I'm someplace where there isn't fish. Like the movies. Or the race track. Not that I don't like meat; it's just that you can't trust anything anymore. Like a machine that can skin fish. How can you beat that? Which I tried to explain to the cop, but she wouldn't listen.

I used to say, "Hamburger." That meant hamburger, which was ground beef. Up the ladder was "Chuck." Hi Chuck. Or Sirloin. SIR Loiiiiiin! Not like Salmon or CATFISH! Then they changed the way they grade beef. They took Prime and made it Choice and Choice and made it Selected Beef, so now the Prime is really the cut above the Prime which you can't get anymore. I keep wondering if the Prime Cows got taken away by space aliens. I mean where did they go? I even called this Chicago outfit and asked them where the Prime Cows went and they didn't know. Day rate it was. Cost me a fortune, it did. All that. I'm here to tell you that computer fish filleter makes me crazy, which is why I end up in the can when I see the sign in the supermarket window.

Get this. It says:

GROUND BEEF
3 Pounds for $1.39 per Pound
Formerly, GROUND CHUCK

This worries me immensely. I can see this cow go into the Bureau of Statistics, or wherever cows go to change their names. "Good Morning. My name's GROUND CHUCK and I'd like to change my name to GROUND BEEF."

So I ask myself, what can I do? I'm a fish guy. I eat fish because I work with fish. It's better except for haddock which is running low because of the pollution and the overfishing. The same goes for clams, scrod and lobsters. I can't believe the farmers up in Maine used to haul lobsters off the shore with pitchforks and use them for fertilizer. So maybe the cow sees what's coming and wants to change his name to GROUND before CHUCK is gone. He's going to end up as FORMERLY anyway. At least I'm going to end up not knowing what kind of cow I'm eating, what to call it, or where to get a job what with the Pisces FK-9000. Which is how I end up in the can.

During my lunch break I take a squid salad in my car to the supermarket so I won't have the growls all afternoon, because once you get cutting fish on Friday you don't get a break. I leave the empty pint container on the seat, take the magic marker from work, whip into the supermarket which for some reason is not too crowded and I waddle on up to the meat department.

There they are. Piles of 3 pounds of FORMERLY GROUND CHUCK at $1.39 per pound.

I mean what do they do, add more fat to CHUCK and make him BEEF? It's all very confusing. I'm here to tell you that *I'm* about to make it unconfusing when I outs with my magic marker and start writing on the labels.

I write like mad. I keep looking over my shoulder. A little old lady with a pink hat with a red feather that sticks out into nowhere, I don't know what kind of feather, shoves me aside and snatches a three pound package that I have yet to re-label. She bangs my ankles with her cart and I nearly faint. She snorts off down the aisle. I write faster. I've got to get all the three pound plus FORMERLY GROUND CHUCK packages.

There must be a hundred and sixty-two packages at least and I'm running out of lunch break, when out of nowhere I see these clerks with red and green aprons coming at me and, in the far corner of my eye I see the brown uniform. I stuff my magic marker in my pocket, but it's no use.

They handcuff me. The manager picks up a 3.4 pound FORMERLY GROUND CHUCK package and shoves it in my face. "What's this?" He looks like he's had a hangover for nineteen days, his face is so red. He points to the label where I have written ALIAS in front of the GROUND BEEF.

"What do you mean, ALIAS?" he says and now the cop is leading me away. "ALIAS, what?" he yells at me.

"FORMERLY GROUND CHUCK! ALIAS GROUND BEEF," I yell over my shoulder and I see the guy is going crazy seeing what I did, which is tell the truth. It's really CHUCK, not BEEF. I wrote at least a hundred ALIAS' on the Ground Beef, three pounds and up. But it doesn't seem to matter, because they run a check on me and find out I'm the guy that got busted in Disneyworld for wearing Goofy's head, which was just lying around the men's room doing nothing. They see I've been to Misdemeanor School, because I've got the card in my wallet right next to my driver's license which has my name and a picture to prove it. I say to the cop, who's six inches shorter than me because she's a she, "How come they don't have a cow's picture on the CHUCK which is now BEEF, but really CHUCK?"

She hauls me outside and sticks me in the back seat of the cruiser. I sit with my wrists burning. Again. I worry about the squid container on the front seat of my car, which will probably get hot and smell, or maybe not, because there's vinegar in it, if I don't get out of jail. Plus, I won't get back to work. I hope they understand. I wonder if the lady with the pink hat and the red feather snitched on me. Her package didn't even have the ALIAS. It goes to show you, nobody's perfect, CHUCK GROUND or otherwise.

Onigiri
by LISA BEATMAN

Roll-square-fold, roll-square-fold. Mariko rolled and squared the lump in her hand, then folded a leaf of *nori* around it. She plumped it down next to its sisters. Pan after pan of neat white rice balls lined up on their metallic beds. Sometimes she felt like a cannibal, sometimes they all did, pale girls queuing up for their afternoon snack, heads stuffed with *kanji*, rounding hips wrapped in the seaweed-green skirt that hung in each of their closets.

Mariko checked her Mickey Mouse watch, it was 14:48, and the gong would ring in precisely one hundred and, she checked her watch again, fourteen seconds. The analog second hand swept imperiously past its digital cousin, doubly ensuring the fidelity of wrist to prompt execution. She narrowed her eyes. That second hand was the boll weevil in the sack of grain that was her life. Mariko dreamed of a place where seconds didn't exist, or if they did, wouldn't matter quite so much. When the homeroom *sensei* assigned pen pals, Mariko always desperately hoped for an American or Mexican one or anyone who didn't have the whorls of time stained so indelibly into their fingers.

Fingerprints. Mariko knew about marks that endure, about the consequence of actions taken before thought was even part of the equation, much less intention. Her very first day of kindergarten, Mariko had shown up two minutes late. The other children were seated quietly in their rows. They had already learned whom they would lead and whom they would follow all the seconds and hours and years until graduation and beyond. Mariko's mother had had to physically pluck her daughter from the television cartoons where she was still sleepily chewing the soft rice of morning. Mariko had clung to the edge of the futon until Mrs. Minami was so exasperated she'd actually slapped her only daughter's face. It was the first and last time she'd surrendered to the *tsunami* wave of emotion, but she knew how much was at stake. Nevertheless, that red mark of shame had remained on Mariko's cheek ever since, the long red imprints of her mother's fingers pointing, like a brand, perpetually at two before eight o'clock.

Mariko yawned, pressing the last ball into place. Head Mistress Miyata would be pleased—each *onigiri* resembled the next, each sticky rice kernel connected to the rest, each smooth ball seated upright in its modest green skirt. But Mariko knew each one had a secret heart. All the girls had their favorites, though they hid any hint of desire well away from the Miss Ichikawas, twin dragon ladies who, it was rumored, were born in the dormitory cellar to a Gakuin student back before the war, and had lived and worked there, molding the student body into respectable, productive citizenry, ever since.

Yes, each girl had her favorite. Mariko was partial to the *umeboshi onigiri*, sucking for hours at the spaces between her teeth where the sour plum paste lingered. She especially craved its thick red essence when her blood ran, in fact, all their blood ran, like a herd of bleeding sheep with the wolves upon them, each month when the moon was split, it was that kind of school. Those quarter-moons, the two long dormitory corridors were like carelessly shaved legs, nicks seeping carmine under the white wadding that could never quite absorb the flow. The maintenance men shook in their boots, stocking up on extra bleach, rubber gloves and boots, just in case it got out of hand. Biohazard, y'know, just can't take too many precautions when it comes to blood, especially that kind of blood, all those feminine pubescent moods eddying about, they could suck a man down just like that.

Gon-n-ng! The kitchen windows rattled with the clack of two hundred thirty-two books slapped shut, the floor vibrating with the shuffle of four hundred sixty-four restless feet. Mariko never had to wonder who would be first in line. Chikako, team captain Chikako, was a tomboy even in her predilection for the simplest, unadorned *onigiri*—just a quick shake of soy sauce, two efficient bites, and she'd be off to practice up her wicked volleyball serve. Kanako, the fearful one, nibbled furtively on the rice ball she snatched up, hoping the green flame of *wasabi* would straighten her spine so she could finally stand up to that bullying *sempai*, Sachiko, from Nagoya. Popular Seiko shared bites of her treasured *natto onigiri* with one and all, cementing intimacies as cohesive and pungent as the fermented soybean mash she favored. You could always count on Seiko to bring people together. The only thing she feared was being alone—one green soybean left behind, chaff in a spent, deserted field. Tomoko—she was the one always to wear her uniform daringly short, so! She could get away with it—dieting had reduced her legs down to the thin, curved weightlessness of the flakes of bonito that coated the half-eaten rice ball she left on the table.

Pudgy Yoko had once tried to make off with Tomoko's leftovers, but the fish-eyed Miss Ichikawas had not only intercepted the contraband rice, but had made Mari stay inside, writing a letter of reflection when all the girls were out enjoying their forty-five minutes of daily free time. Why had she transgressed the most basic principles of Gakuin Girl's School, of Japanese society? What had been the results of her actions? How many people had Mari inconvenienced, like the Miss Ichikawas who had to read and reread each of Mari's drafts until she had clearly spelled out her remorse, tears and blood smudging the lined and frantically scratched out analysis of her lack of control, the last draft dropped by Ichikawa claws into the *"Hanseibun"* file that would trail Mari like a bad dog throughout her life?

"One Ball per Student," *Ichi Onigiri Gakuin-wa*. This, the Gakuin School motto, hung over the gates as well as the double doors to the honeycomb of dormitory cells. "Ichi Onigiri Gakuin-wa" had been kneaded and rolled into each Gakuin student until it held them together like *kirin* in sweet-ferment community, the hard individual kernels becoming pliant and banding together in fluent starchiness. One Ball per Girl—this dictum ensured pan after pan of white and green uniformity, slim girls whose hips girded no surprises, rows and rows of feminine oneness, Future Wives, Future Office Ladies of Japan, no head sticking up vulnerable to the hungry mouth of the outsider…

Mariko pulled straight a damp lock of hair that was threatening to curl in the humid vapor rising from the industrial rice-cooker before her. Would she ever see the bottom? Was this her life, all that it would be, was she only a faceless, bodiless hand shaping what had come and what would come, or worse, was she only the empty space between curved hand and blob of rice, only that empty space?

Mariko suddenly trembled—she was that hungry mouth. Before she understood what her left hand had done, it had seized the last *onigiri* she had formed and stuffed it down the tight elastic waistband, down past the green pleats, the white cotton, down to rest, smeared against her rumbling belly, the *nori* stuck like grass growing wild, the white and red paste joining with the rising stink of her full womanhood, to wait for a time (when?) till she was alone (where?), and she could finally eat her fill.

Late that night when her roommate Yuko was bathing in the communal *ofuro*, Mariko, legs folded under her knees on the floor of their little room, turned the alarm clock face against the wall, and began to write in a spatter of brushstrokes, "Dear Juanita…"

Grocery Store Diva: Three Poems
by Carly Sachs

Vegetables Aren't Immaculately Conceived

Ramona likes to nail her name on people's foreheads
at the farmer's market. She's got everyone entranced,
except the corn cobbler who calls her a slut
because she wears daisy duke overalls
and talks shop with the tomato pushers and plum fairies,
and somehow ends up in their beds.

She knows it's not right to sleep with them
because they always end up giving her free produce,
but that's not her motivation.
She does it to be close to the earth.
She prefers them to leave the dirt under their nails,
their bodies baked in sweat and grass.

She dreams of birthing radishes and sweet peppers instead of children.
She imagines potatoes and carrots floating around her uterus.
She rubs her belly and thinks of soup.

On the news last night, Ramona heard about the famine in India.
She thinks if she could learn their language
and sleep with their farmers,
she could be popping produce from between her legs in no time.

Think of all the money that could be saved on irrigation!
she exclaims to the empty room. Fertility goddess Ramona,
it has a nice ring to it. I'll be right up there,

slapping high five's with Krishna.
So the next time she sees the corn cobbler, instead of ignoring him, she'll snap back, Your golden ears are bastard children!

The Crisis

Something about a bag is trust.
It is comforting to know
that you will be the first person to open its contents.
In this city, security is everything.
Ramona is playing it safe.
She questions what organic actually means.
She buys more pre-packaged food than she used to
because she saw something that no one should ever see.
One day while walking down 5th Avenue, she saw the owner
of the Regal Market spit-shining his apples. He'd pick them up
one by one, lift them to his mouth then
rub them on his apron and then put them back.
And there were customers buying these apples as if
la la this is normal. Moments like these make Ramona
re-examine her values. She remembers when she protested
canned vegetables. But the cans kept the produce safe from
grubby, disgusting store owners.
But, on the other hand,
the consumer is robbed of having something fresh and
tasting like Mother Earth and given something with preservatives
and who knows what else. Ramona continues her list of pros and
cons on her way to the Farmer's Market.
It's beginning to make her head hurt.
All around her she sees people fondling rutabagas and turnips.
They wipe their noses, then pick up five peaches
before finding the one they want.
But then, who knows what the people at the canning facilities are like.
What if they haven't bathed? What if they put their hairs

in the string beans? For the first time in her life,
Ramona feels betrayed, vulnerable.
She runs around the market frantic, not knowing what to do.
She thinks about going out to eat,
but then she faces the same dilemma, only magnified
because there are more people involved, the cook, the waiter.
Pull yourself together she tells herself. You can't stop eating.
For a second she thinks about the bulimic girl she followed
around in the Giant Eagle. I wonder if she had these thoughts
and that's what lead to her eating disorder.
Ramona remembers the girl always buying cheese.
There is something comforting in that.
Ramona heads over to the Amish dairy.
After all, she thinks, how can you be skeptical
of an Amish man and his cheese?

Ramona's Mantra

is "if I can't pronounce it, maybe I shouldn't eat it"
which she lifted from a DiPrima poem.
This includes most pre-packaged foods
since they have ingredients more than four syllables.
Monosodium whose-a-fates and alpha omega triglycerides
are persona-non-grata in her kitchen.
She figures that food she can't pronounce must be immoral
and will eventually kill you if you eat enough of it.
She's started a list of offenders. So far she's blacklisted
Ho-Ho's, Spam, and Cheez Whiz for inappropriate
sexual language, attempting to engineer meat, and
poor spelling. Before grocery shopping she sits zazen
and talks to the simple spirits of squash and wheat
asking for strength and guidance. By the time
she gets to the store, she is still chanting, "Beets, no meats.
Lentils are credentials. I want veggies, processed food

is worse than wegies!" But since she's a New Yorker,
no one pays any attention. They've all got their own
issues. She passes a man near the produce chanting,
"Potatoes and tomatoes, I'm going to get laid-os!"
Ramona continues her shopping, envisioning macrobiotic
and antibiotic meals. She's also trying to buy foods
that rhyme. It's a game she made up to entertain herself
and it cuts down on excess products that she has to lug
back to her fifth floor walk-up. So far in her basket
she has greens, beans, garlic, beverages (alcoholic),
kitchen cleaner, tofu wieners, rigatoni, macaroni,
pineapple juice and couscous. She heads back
to the ethnic food aisle hoping to find something
that rhymes with ice cream when she runs into
the tomato and potato guy's girlfriend. She's practically
singing, "Tomatoes and potatoes. He thinks sex,
I said Tex-Mex. Ole!"

Memoir of a Utensil Meal,
or Recipe for Old-Fashioned Macaroni and Cheese

by Mina Samuels

When I was growing up my father didn't travel a lot. He didn't even go to a real office, at least not what I thought of as an office then, something accessed by elevator in a tall building where the windows didn't open and secretaries glided around hushed halls. My father taught at the university in my hometown, and the place he worked was more like a library with a desk in the basement of an old stone building. My two younger brothers and I would walk over to visit my dad and usually we arrived in his office by climbing into the window well, tapping on the leaded glass panes to make our presence known, and waiting for my dad to crank open the window. On warmer days the window was already open and we would see if we could sneak through it without our father noticing our arrival. Even if someone was in his office, he would just give us a selection of the Lego or art supplies he kept in the bottom drawer of his desk and send us out into the hall to play until he was finished with his meeting. At the time I didn't know how special this was, the casualness of our arrivals at my father's workplace, his unquestionable happiness to see us.

Because in other ways he was a more typical patriarch, autocratic and prone to laying down the law at home. He had rules for most everything, not just bedtime and how much television we could watch. Clean towels, for example, had to be folded lengthwise in three and then three again, to form a neat rectangle before going into the linen cupboard. And, of course, he expected my mother to do all the shopping, the cooking, and the cleaning. Dinner was served, according to his wishes, at exactly 6:30 p.m. Any later and he would begin hovering in the kitchen, as if he might starve to death in the next minutes before my mother got food on the table, and then wouldn't there be repercussions down the line.

Whenever I catch myself hardening into a routine, I never wonder where the tendency came from. My dad had specific ideas of what constituted an evening meal, too. There had to be meat or fish, preferably meat, a vegetable, and a starch, meaning rice or potatoes. My mother too had her mealtime rules. Girls set the table, which meant me, and it had to be just so. The telephone was never answered during meals, even though we had no answering machine, and everyone ate together. I always envied families where a variety of siblings and their friends seemed to cruise through around meal time and forage for themselves, joining others already at the table, eating straight out of Tupperware standing up, coming and going on their own schedules.

Three or four times a year my father would go away for a few days, to a conference of other professors, or meetings of one or another of the associations he belonged to. I remember the Canadian Professors for Peace in the Middle East best, CPPME, which my mother called CPPPPP-me. When my father was away it was as if not only he had gone, but my mother too. Mum became a different person. Rules were relaxed. We might not clean our toys up every single night. We might not fold our laundry, but instead just use it straight from the clean laundry basket.

What I remember most though is meals. We hardly ever ate meat and vegetables, except wieners and beans. Pasta was pulled from the back shelves and served almost nightly. We swirled spaghetti in thick meatless tomato sauce, laughing at each other's red-rimmed lips. And we ate heaping mounds of homemade macaroni and cheese, which my mother called mac & tac, seeing who could stretch out a cheesy string the farthest. My middle brother once reached a thin gooey line of pale orange melted cheese clear across the table, passing his fork on to me, at which point the string broke and even after my father was back we could see tiny flecks of dried cheese on the placemats, which just wouldn't wash out.

And every time my father was away we had a 'one utensil meal.' It was my mother's invention, and I have never found another person who has had one. When the macaroni and cheese went into the oven, my mother would fill a paper grocery bag with an assortment of cooking utensils—giant wooden spoon, cheese grater, hand-held meat grinder, whisk, spatula, hand beater, measuring cup, tongs, and whatever else struck her fancy. My brothers and I were each blindfolded in turn and reached inside the bag. The first thing our hand touched was our utensil, which meant that one of us might eat our whole dinner of macaroni and cheese with a whisk.

I remember once trying to see if I could use the hand beater to spin food into my mouth. I learned that you can spin food everywhere, except into your mouth. Even cleaning up a mess of macaroni sticking to chairs, floors and walls felt nothing like a chore, and our stomachs often hurt from gasping with hilarity.

In my memory of those meals we lived for a moment outside of our world. We performed a strange ritual that was all our own, which served no purpose but joy.

❧

Old-fashioned and available in hip diners everywhere, nothing instant or fake about it, here is the recipe for mac & tac. What utensil you eat it with is your choice.

Old-Fashioned Macaroni & Cheese

INGREDIENTS:

- 2 tbsp butter
- 2 tbsp flour
- 1 cup milk
- 2 cups grated cheese (Cheddar, Mozzarella or Swiss are favorites, but Goat cheese, Blue cheese, Parmesan, Romano or Asiago can also be mixed in)
- Salt and Pepper
- 1 tsp dried basil
- 1 lb pasta—macaroni elbows, fusilli or bowties (leftovers are always great)

• Preheat the oven to 350 degrees F.

• Put a large pot of water on to boil for the pasta. When the water boils add the pasta. Be careful not to overcook. Set a timer for 8 minutes, if necessary. When the pasta is done, drain, but don't rinse.

- Meanwhile melt the butter in a large saucepan. Add flour a half spoon at a time until a thick paste is formed. Pour the milk in slowly, stirring constantly until the paste and milk are well mixed and the milk is bubbling slightly. Do not boil the milk.

- Add the grated cheese gradually, stirring slowly and evenly as the cheese melts. Keep adding cheese until the sauce reaches the level of thickness you like.

- Add salt and pepper to taste. Sprinkle in the dried basil.

- Transfer the drained pasta back into the pasta pot, and pour over the cheese sauce. Mix thoroughly. Optional: Here you can add cooked cubes of the winter vegetable of your choice, butternut squash for example, or brussel sprouts, if your taste buds (like mine) run in that direction.

- Put the macaroni and cheese mixture into a casserole. Sprinkle grated cheeses over the top (lots is good), bread crumbs too if you like, though I have always been a cheese-only purist. Cover the casserole.

- Place the dish in the preheated oven for 30 minutes. You can leave it longer, but turn the heat down to 250 to keep it warm.

- Serve up with wine (red or white—remember there are no rules), beer, and lots of good conversation.

The Absence of Everything Else
by Douglas W. Milliken

Through crunching roads packed stiff with snow: it was well past two when we arrived back to Angela's apartment, the duplex she shares with five others. Moonlight blued the ground, the trees, houses and street signs. Blurry and cold, a world simplified with snow. Stepping silently inside, hungry, we peeled away jackets and fumbled with snowy shoes.

Nick and Emily had put on a good feed—teriyaki roast turkey, steamed broccoli, spiced mashed potatoes, boats of gooey ice cream—but that was hours ago: horror movies and politics rebuild an appetite. Softly, quickly, we crept to the kitchen like thieves into a vault.

The fridge was no good. We took swigs of seltzer from the bottle—"Mmm," she said, "fizzy"—but the bubbles only encouraged our stomachs' self-digestion. No fruit in the crisper, no crackers, not even a stale rice cake forgotten in the cupboard. Nothing, least of all anything we wanted.

Angela clutched her belly and faked a moan—"Ohh!"—then straightened and did a wiggling dance. "I must pee." Socks whispering on linoleum, she wriggled into the bathroom and closed the door.

In her absence, I repeated my orbit, cycling between fridge, freezer, cupboards, then back. Nothing. I checked the pots on the stove. Nothing. Then I remembered the paper grocery bag on the counter—the one now hidden behind her roommates' abandoned bottles of Tanqueray and tonic water, dissected limes—and the few things we'd picked up from the natural foods store in town. The sparkling cider and cranberry nectar we brought to Nick and Em's dinner, but the rest…

When Angela came out from the bathroom, I was standing with a knife at the counter, measuredly cubing a thick organic fudge brownie, its cellophane wrapper splayed beneath it like a shroud. "You're good," she said silkily, sidling up against me. "Real good."

"Shh." I fed her a piece of brownie. Her lips closed over my fingertips. "They're sleeping."

Standing quietly hip-to-hip, we ate the brownie and looked out the kitchen window above the sink at the black shape of the cat lady's house next door, hoping to catch a glimpse of her tabby or coon or Siamese or whatever but seeing nothing. High above and beyond our view, the moon glowed fat and pale like a drunken rich uncle, basking gregarious above the sleeping world blanketed below. The moment passed in perfect silence, perfect stillness, just two people watching nothing and eating bits of chocolate. Then we brushed our teeth, turned out the lights, stripped down to winter goose-fleshed skins and, bound in covers and arms, slept.

Chinese Restaurant Suite
by Richard Berlin

1. Blue Teapot

The streets of Chinatown fall toward the bay,
fog drifting over Alcatraz like an uncertain lover.
In the commotion outside, bent shoulders
lurch past with fresh chickens, black beans,
baby bok choy, oyster sauce and lotus root.
I sip jasmine tea and study the teapot's blue
lovers fleeing across the final bridge.
The waiter knows me well, brings a bowl
filled with shitakes, golden ginger threads,
white noodles wide as a woman's finger,
green scallions cut into wedding rings,
prawns with whiskered faces and empty eyes.
My chopsticks pierce the surface,
grasp the firm resistance of ginger,
each bite hot and salty as her taste.
Flowery steam, a sip of tea,
the gentle kiss of cup and marble,
and a world disappears in fog.

2. Dim Sum for One

They crowd me in a clatter of bus buckets
and fish tank hum, crammed close
to CO_2 cartridges and cases of Coke.
Waiters cart chow mei, spring rolls,

shrimp buns and broccoli
in portions for three or four,
all grown cold before they reach me
at the far circle of the dining room.
On the wall, a golden dragon
inhales cigarette smoke from men
presiding at tables of eight,
plates piled with steaming noodles,
their chopsticks probing the warmth.
Suddenly, the sound system blasts
Happy Birthday in Chinese
backed by an oompah band,
and I wonder, Who am I without my family?
almost invisible in a corner,
the huge steel pot of jasmine tea
grown bitter as it steeps,
a man with portions too big for his plate.

3. Foreign Family

Dragons in every doorway,
drumbeats on the street,
a New Year's crowd thicker than blood,
or corn-starched bean thread soup.
We duck the masses for Shanghai—
wife, daughter, new boyfriend.
Blackboard in Mandarin,
bone marrow on our neighbor's plate,
we manage long beans in black vinegar
and steaming dumplings.
White cabbage arrives with red chilis,
an order of tea-smoked whitefish,
and a mound of sweet red bean cakes,
gifts our family eats like astronauts

savoring their last meal on earth.
But her boyfriend stares like a sightseer
at feeding time for the seals.
When he asks for a fork
the waiter brings fresh chopsticks.

Sweet Potatoes
by Elizabeth Anne Socolow

With relative innocence, a daughter in late middle age is distracting her father in his nineties. He sits, spending his days gumming food in a toothless mouth, reading little, writing some, hearing poorly, and still joyous to be alive, watching the birds light on the very tall, skinny trees in the back courtyard. The day his daughter visits, he does not want his sweet potatoes. His wife is worried about his lunch. She is concerned that he is not eating. His food will get cold. This is a second, late marriage of deep affection, his wife the comfort of his widower solitude, and not his daughter's mother. His daughter is at least sixty when this is taking place on the Upper East Side of Manhattan in the spring of 2001, a time, generally, of relative innocence. He will be gone before September, will never know the destruction of his lawyers' office building, his will sucked out the windows of Liberty Place.

The daughter has gone with some widows to see the Chardin exhibit. The others went on to the Planetarium, the new exhibits in the new building, just opened. She has come to see her father, dying, bringing a postcard of the boy blowing soap bubbles for his younger brother. Her father wants only to study the postcard; he will not eat his food, sweet potatoes, so beautifully mashed, so wonderfully colored. But no, he wants to hear about the Chardin exhibit at the Met. He has never heard of Chardin, though he has lived all his adult life in the vicinity of Fifth Avenue, walked to the Museum at least hundreds of times, and there is something he does not know, a painter he has never seen.

—*French*, he says. *Tell me. Show me.* Life has a new thing in it. Though he could not say so, he feels young.

—Chardin flourished in the years just after Newton's death, his daughter says.

—*His name, again, you told me, tell me again,* her father answers.

—Chardin, she says, punching the word as she has learned to do so that he can hear, not saying it loud, not screaming.—Jean Siméon Chardin.

Her father repeats: —*Jean Siméon Chardin. Look at the bubble. He catches its thinness. The thinness of soap bubbles. Almost without gravity. A sphere unlike Newton's heavenly ones. It's a kind of anti-Newton joke. So light. Almost weightless. And the little one behind him. Has a hat. It must be cold. But there are green leaves, a kind of ivy, do you think? Growing around the window. What do you think? Is it real; or an allegory?* Twenty years have fallen away. This is the man her father had been. His close friend was Leonard K. who lectured on Caravaggio and taught at _____.

This is the curiosity and observation she once knew, the scientist and painter; this is who raised her. His wife is pursing her lips. Time is getting away from her. She is angry that these sudden windows of clarity and wit come not from dailiness but from newness. The daughter gets all the good parts. She takes time out to go to the museum. There is a tension in the room of which the old man is oblivious, so caught is he in the painting.

—*He wears his hair like Mozart,* he says.—*Or a wig. Do you think the hair stylists from Paris traveled to Salzburg and designed all the same wigs, all from the fashion capital of Europe? What do you think? But look at the patience in the breath, and the little bulge, it is not a perfectly symmetric bubble, the way they are not in real life. Imperfect, so real. Swelling, in the process of finding its true form. Like the little one, brother or is it a sister? In the background so indistinct but focused on the big one. Coming into his own. Taking his form, like the bubble. You can almost feel that he must be on tiptoe, standing as tall as possible to see. What makes that impression? The way the eyes are looking, but half closed as if straining to look, and keep balance on tiptoe at the same time. Amazing. And the good example. The bigger one, do you think it could be a very young father, blowing out the window, on the ledge of it, not to make the floor slippery? Or wet the carpet? What a picture! This is a wonderful postcard you have brought me. Chardin. What did you tell me his first names were?*

—Arthur, you must eat your lunch. Your sweet potatoes, fixed the way you like them, his wife insists.

—Dr. W., the beautiful nurse cajoles in her Island accent,—You must do what your wonderful wife is telling you. You must put your postcard down. It is not going to walk anywhere. (She laughs.) And then, when you finish your sweet potatoes, you can look at it.

Sweet potatoes are an old person's food. Mash them and they have tremendous nutrient value; add an egg or milk or one of the liquid diet supplements old people rely on, and they are a colorful alternative to the all white diet of farina, potatoes, vanilla pudding.

A terrible smile comes over the face of the old man being forced to put down the postcard. He is three years old. He is ninety-two years old.—*If you tell me,* he says in a very quiet voice, the same thoughtful voice with which he spoke to the man who used to be his close friend, was once his patient, whose life he saved and, for the saving, was rewarded with years of conversations about art,—*if you tell me the name of sweet potato in French, the way Chardin might have had to eat his sweet potatoes, or refuse them, then I will eat them.*

—O my goodness, Dr. W. You are full of mischief.

—Arthur, this is not a game of Rumplestiltskin. You need your nourishment. You can't live on the light coming off a picture or spun flax. We're not living in a fairy tale here. The wife sits still, exasperated.

Of course, the daughter, my friend, who could not be less than sixty, is obedient, the first child, searching all over the book cases in the den, the living room, the porch alcove, for a French dictionary. *Je sême a tout vent,* the Larousse used to say. I sow in all winds, and the engraved frontispiece of the girl blowing the dandelion gone to seed was as gossamer as the bubble in the Chardin painting. *Larousse illustrée,* la ruse. It is nowhere to be found. Probably she took it from this home when she went to college. What seeds is she sowing now in her father's mind, what seeds of dissension toward her stepmother? What will be the outcome of this deviation in routine, this one excursion with the widows to see something other than her father, for two hours only on a Saturday morning?

In all the house of many dictionaries, there are none that define sweet potato in French, only yam.—*L'igname,* she tells her father from a miniature book, not two inches high, covered in red leather.—*L'igname* means yam, but NOT sweet potato.

L'igname, he says, fully himself again, ordinary voice, no coyness, no ruse, just rumination, deep, clear, all connections in order.—*That means no name. How extraordinary. Of all the things in the world to say this is the one that has no name. Why a sweet potato? Why would it be the nameless thing? Where did the French bring them from, lovey?* He says this to his wife.

—Africa. The French had colonies in Africa. And the Belgians, who speak French, did. But long after Chardin. Didn't you say he was a Mozart contemporary, Rosalie? But it doesn't really matter when it was, does it? Except that Chardin almost surely could not have painted sweet potatoes or eaten them. Unless they also come from India. Unless they were brought back before the French colonies were established. Maybe the African word for sweet potato, or yam, sounds like 'igname.' 'Yigname.' 'Ignamini.' Ignominy. I don't know. Cognate, is that the right word, Rosalie? She says this to the daughter.

—*Right,* her husband answers, on his toes.—*Well, my love. I see you are enjoying this too. It gives the mind a workout, does it not? Rosie, my love, I am so glad you brought me this postcard.*

Rosalie is aware that it does not sit well with her stepmother when they are both addressed as love, though surely the world has room for more than one kind of affection. She is aware that soon her mother will start talking about eating again, that by now the potatoes are cold, and that her mother is rigid like this because if her father is ninety-two, his wife is eighty-seven. She is entitled.

—*What power,* her father asks, *does a sweet potato have that they were afraid to name it? Let me eat them, I will see if I can taste the answer. Very like Lear, don't you think? But this postcard has saved me from his fate. Chardin. A new thing in the world.*

His wife relaxes. His nurse feeds him. His daughter wonders and will wonder into his death, and after it, where she can find someone who can tell her about sweet potatoes, their power, the thing that cannot be named. She does not think of doing a Google search until after a chance conversation on a city bus with a young man who knows botany, who was carrying a book called *Flora of Mexico* on his lap, and whom she engaged in conversation about sweet potatoes, as they rode through a traffic jam near the crosstown streets leading to the Queensborough Bridge. The young man had said something half to himself, as they stood in the bus, becalmed near the Plaza Hotel. He seemed both relaxed and tense, eager to get to wherever he was going, but easy in time. When she asked him if he was in a hurry, and what had he said, and had he spoken to her, he said he yearly was in the jungles of Costa Rica doing fieldwork, and there and in the rain forests time has a different quality, of course, and he tried, he said, to carry that time to traffic jams, but the honking and the tension of others in the bus made it difficult altogether to forget the rush of cities. Rosalie asked him what he did fieldwork in and he said:

—*I study ferns, I'm a botanist,* so she asked him about sweet potatoes and yams in Africa and the New World. Was there any reason he could think of that they would be called in French, *l'igname,* the nameless thing.

He was eager to say that sweet potatoes are altogether different from yams, and that he was no expert.—I know a little about yams. In particular, the wild ones, he told her. The wild ones have something of a reputation. *Dioscorea* is their botanical name, and we now know they're packed with precursors of hormones and steroids. We know they were used to cast spells in both Africa and Latin America, and for soap and stunning animals, fish, I think, maybe rodents.

The bus stood still and thousands of children, it seemed, crossed the street with their parents on the way to the still extant Fifth Avenue F. A. O. Schwarz, and then, to beguile the time waiting in the bus, its engine roaring, the man with the book gave her the story of his mother in the state of Oaxaca in Mexico in 1964. Stories like this from his mother led him to botany, he said. Rosalie judged him to be in his thirties, perhaps late thirties. She told him about her father, dying, and so keenly wanting to know why in French yam is 'the nameless thing.'—*Well, those hormone-like substances are powerful. Some of them were used in the sixties in the first birth control pills. Wild yams in fact were used in tropical mountainous regions to cast spells. The tuber had nameless power and the story goes it was used to poison enemies. Sometimes the toxins acted so forcefully that children were never born to those who partook. They stunned fish, made soap, killed rodents, and ended fertility in cultures where it was the main thing. Dioscorea, the wild yams, inspired fear for what they could accomplish. No one ordinarily knows these things, except experts. That the French who met the thing and communicated with the people who used it, called it the nameless thing, would argue that they either translated its native name, or understood from their conversations that people are afraid to name the thing that awes. Like the ancient Hebrews not naming God. How the ordinary eating yams come to be named the same thing as the awe inspiring wild ones, I can't guess, except for the gross botanical resemblances. No one in the West eats wild yams.*

But I am ahead of my story. The old man is not yet gone, and Rosalie knows nothing of why a yam is called *l'igname*. She never got to tell her father about the wild yam and birth control pills and the name of God. The next postcard she brought him, after Chardin, the last, was also about food. She told me:

—My father's last birthday at Easter, the Pascal lamb, the Last Supper, Passover table. I brought him a postcard of the famous painting.

—*Where is my mother in the picture, and my sisters Ethel and Rita?* he wanted to know.—*You would think*, he said, *if I'm like this, my father would come to my sickbed.*

—Your father wanted to come but could not get here, Rosalie told him.

It is so hard to travel to this city. Given her answer, it was fitting, it seemed to me, that in a traffic jam, she learned a year later, the answer to his question about the ineffable name of yams, and learned, too, the longing and the letting go, the mystery of the thing not told.

Watching Him Cook
by Meredith Escudier

The man I love cooks. He does this with Japanese knives and extra long chopsticks, with wooden spoons and rubber spatulas and with his hands, his heart and his body. He is close to the food. He seems to enter it and become part of it and as he does so I can see the boundaries blurring between him and nature's bounty. He is the silvery fish being rinsed under cold water, its purple gills and shining eyes bringing the promise of freshness. He is the dark green Italian parsley, even as he pulls it apart, breaking off the stems before chopping and adding lemon juice for a Lebanese tabbouleh. Sicilian tomatoes, moist buffalo cheese, tender basil, ribbons of yellow olive oil, clumps of white spring onions, handfuls of mushrooms still smelling of earth, he is all of these. Zen-like, he handles his charges with quiet respect, meditating on their essence as he coaxes them along, helping them release their own fragrances, colors, flavors…their inherent beauty.

I watch him. I photograph him. I inch my way around the kitchen looking for interesting angles as I try to document this act of oneness. I catch the denim shirt, the floured hands, the translucent onions. But I know I am intruding. "You're a wizard, a magician, a genius," I effuse. He responds with a pale smile and shakes his head. Recognition is not part of the deal.

The house fills with a combination of odors. A hint of ginger melts into candied endives. Curried onions sharpen the air. Simmering, darkening eggplant blends into a whiff of garlic. I get it. The Mediterranean. That is where we belong, seated on an upstairs terrace of a white stucco home in Greece, overlooking the boats as they float along the horizon. An occasional breeze refreshes our spirits on this scorcher of a day. The air shimmers.

Or maybe it is tamari sauce and squid, crushed red pepper or green horseradishy mustard. We're in Japan. I see myself attired in exquisite silks falling in folds around my ankles. I crunch away on morsels of squid, my unyielding mandibles fierce and carnivorous, despite delicately painted lips.

Or my plate offers up stringy beef of dripping Mexican machaca, enlivened by hot chiles inflaming our tongues and palates until the greasiness of moist avocado and corn tortillas softens and rebalances them once again. We are peasants, *campesinos*, and proud of it. I'll have my baby in the fields, tie up the umbilical cord with all the efficiency of a well-observed, timeworn gesture, only to make dinner on an open fire for my expanding family.

Or could it be *confit de canard?* The man I love is French after all, and we might well find familiar comfort from the southwest of France, where ducks and geese have been lovingly forcefed by women who wear navy-blue satinet aprons and clunk around in wooden shoes over felt slippers. Tenderly, even sympathetically, they will slaughter their poultry and conserve them in grease, so that we, on an off-day, might sit and enjoy the rich, dark flesh of these almost gamey birds. We sauté potatoes, heavy on garlic and parsley. We can't help it. Only potatoes from deepest, rural Périgord can truly accompany confit.

Finishing *en grande beauté* comes an array of tropical fruit, cut up and served on a tray, sushi-style: juicy African pineapples, wedges of mango and papaya, Chinese lychees topped by a curlicue of their partially-peeled skin, inviting us to reach out and pop them into our mouths. We're back in Florida, fighting the squirrels for the plumpest mango. The air is steamy and mockingbirds nervily defend their chirping young. Fruit flies, gnats, unwanted insects dance around our faces. We swish them away in a gesture of futility.

But I digress. It is not the end result that counts for this man who cooks. It is not this work of temporary art adorning my table or your table. Nor is it truly the voyage. Instead, it is the process, the meditation, the communication. It is the singing, simmering celery root that causes the man I love to return time and again to his cast iron pan and formulate the essential question: *"alors…what is this saying?"* A quiet, self-sufficient, private, inner-directed man is in intimate, maybe mysterious, communication with food.

"You should open a restaurant," many a dinner guest has exclaimed. The man I love winces quietly, knowing he would not cook for unknown people with rhythmically regular requests. He could not do it. He prefers to confine himself to a circle of a few: family, friends, the gourmet and the gourmand, the lover of good things, the receiver of warm and creative energies, the depleted, the wanting, the hopeful.

I think I understand now. This man who cooks…loves.

Almond and Chocolate
by Cortney Davis

The day my pregnant daughter's blood test comes back negative
(no risk of cystic fibrosis in her unborn girl)
a present arrives in the mail from my friend Jeanne,
a book of poems mixed in with the Christmas blessings and bills.
The book is good, poems that make my eyes sting
like a fresh-cut onion would, words like onion slices
sizzling in butter: pungent, transparent.

I'm not slicing onions today, but I am baking a cake
for the folks at the post office, and in between baking I read the book
all the way through. At the end of section three
nine poems are tacked on, gifts a reader wouldn't get to
unless she loved the book's beginning,
which I do, so I keep reading, mixing the cake and wiping my eyes.

These last poems are about the author's daughter, Sarah,
and her diagnosis—the way cystic fibrosis
clogs her lungs, twists her bowel. How, because *it's always fatal*,
Sarah thinks that forty years of it,
of almost anything, might just be wonderful.

I stop beating the eggs, stop pouring batter
into my aluminum pan, so dented that cakes come out imperfect
but delicious, and go down on my knees in thanks for our luck
and in grief for the poet and her daughter.
Upstairs, hidden, are presents for my grandchild,
more than I should buy, my daughter will say,
spoiling her. I close this book,

this disease my unborn granddaughter will never, ever have—
and the cake rises, the kitchen fills
with the smell of relief, of guilt,
which for today God has chosen almond and chocolate.

Hawaiian Tooth
by OLIVER SACKS

Though I'm falling apart a bit now, I always had excellent teeth—or did have until a few years ago. I had no suspicion that anything was the matter until I went for my twice-a-year check-up. I opened my mouth proudly, expecting Alan, my dentist, to offer his usual congratulations, but the moment he saw my teeth he exclaimed sharply, and drew back with a look of horror. What had he seen, I wondered. What could justify such a look? Maggots? Aliens?

"What have you been doing?" Alan demanded.

His question disturbed me, made me anxious, guilty. I thought of my sins, my peccadilloes—could masturbation (for example) have produced a dental catastrophe?

"Could you be a little more specific?" I asked, gulping.

"Sure," he answered. "Have you gone ape over pineapple?"

"Yes," I stuttered. "I suppose I have. I've been on a diet of cottage cheese and pineapple for the last month. I've been eating five or six pineapples a day. But how did you guess?"

"I saw this other patient," he said. (Alan always likes to answer a question with a story.) "She'd gone to Hawaii and for three weeks straight gorged herself on tropical fruit, mostly pineapple. And when she came back she had what you have—little craters on top of some of the teeth—the enamel eaten clear away... Bromelin. A proteolytic enzyme in pineapples...nasty stuff. Half the people of

---

Copyright © 2005 by Oliver Sacks
Printed with the permission of the Wylie Agency

Hawaii have it. Dentists call it 'Hawaiian Tooth.'"

Craters. It sounded menacing. "What do the craters look like?" I asked, curiously, picturing a pock-marked moonscape.

"I'll show you," said Alan. He pivoted the big dental camera into place and took several exposures. "Isn't that neat?" he exclaimed, unpeeling the Polaroids a minute later. "Looks like they've been punched out with a die."

I looked at the photos with mixed fascination and disgust—the pathologist looking at his own pathology, the wounded doctor examining his own wounds.

"Great photos," said Alan. "Striking story. Let's publish it. We'll call it 'Hawaiian Tooth.'" (Alan and I had co-authored papers in the Annals of Dentistry.)

"That's fine," I said. "But what about my teeth? Will the enamel grow back?"

"No," said Alan. "But it won't get worse. You can still eat pineapple, but eat it in moderation—why must you do everything in excess?—and make sure you use a toothpick, floss, clean your teeth straight away. And perhaps a mildly alkaline mouthwash afterwards."

The thought of these elaborate precautions, and the wicked little craters in my teeth, all but stopped me eating pineapples for several years. But now I have gone back to them, at least in moderation, always following Alan's instructions to the letter. My teeth, all thirty-two of them, are perfect once again—apart from some tiny apical craters which no one can see and no one knows about but my dentist and me.

Bon Appetit
by Peter Gray

"*Zut alors!* What is that horrible noise?" Jacques exclaimed.

"The cicadas have emerged from their 17-year hibernation, *mon cher*," replied his wife Jacqueline.

Jacques stepped out on his backyard deck to take a closer look. As he gaped in astonishment at the swarm of buzzing insects, a cicada flew into his mouth. He was about to spit it out, but paused when he tasted a pleasant, slightly nutty flavor. "*C'est bon*," he said with his mouth full. "You must try this, *mon amour*."

Jacqueline was game. She had tasted snails, ants, spiders, bees and other insects. "Too bland, *mon cheri*, it needs flavoring. Why don't we create some new recipes and serve cicadas in our restaurant?"

The couple owned Chez Flora, the only pan-Eurasian vegan restaurant in the area. But recently, many of their regular customers had become carnivores, and their business was in danger of failing.

"*Bon*," said Jacques, "we must hurry and gather as many newly hatched cicadas as possible. We can serve some of them fresh now and freeze the rest for later eating."

"But won't our customers be disgusted by large insects staring at them with bulging red eyes, six hairy legs, and veined wings?"

"We'll remove the heads, shells, wings and legs, so they will look like shrimp, but taste much better."

That evening they sat down at the kitchen table to prepare the menu. "For hors d'oeuvre, we could marinate the cicadas in white wine and Dijon mustard, bread and crisp fry them," Jacqueline said.

"*Très bien!* I could make a cream of cicada soup with avocado and morels."

"For the salad we could prepare an ensemble of singing cricket, grasshopper and cicada au gratin, on a bed of spring greens, and call it 'The Three Tenors.'"

"*Formidable!* As an entrée, soft-shelled, jumbo sautéed cicadas in a white wine and butter reduction. We could also offer curried cicadas on a bed of basmati rice. And for a third entrée, a baked lobster stuffed with a ragout of cicadas, raisins and pine nuts."

"What about a wine to go with the entrees?"

"A 1987 *Macon-Charney* would be apropos, since it coincides with the 17-year life cycle of the cicada. And for the grand finale, chocolate covered cicadas with raspberries, cicada crepes in a Grand Marnier sauce, or a cicada gateau."

A few days later, after successfully trying out the dishes on their friends and relatives, Jacqueline sent a copy of the new menu, with an invitation to dinner, to the media food critics. All were greatly impressed. "Chez Flora deserves four stars for its delicious, nutritious and creative menu," raved one reviewer. "You may never experience fine French dining like this *tout le monde*."

"Chefs Jacques and Jacqueline have created a tour de force. The entrees have been prepared with élan, the desserts with éclat, and the appetizers with finesse. We highly recommend this restaurant to connoisseurs, gourmands, gourmets and even the bourgeois diner," wrote another.

"For sophisticated diners interested in healthy and tasty food, we suggest Chez Flora," a third critic remarked. "Cicadas are a safer alternative source of protein than beef, pork, chicken or fish."

Following these and similarly boffo reviews, the phone rang constantly, and prospective diners had to make dinner reservations four to six weeks in advance. The culinary couple contracted with Random House for an illustrated cookbook, and demonstrated their skills with the skillet on national television.

One day, a severe thunderstorm caused a massive power outage, and the restaurant did not have a backup generator for its freezers. The public would have to wait until the year 2021 to taste cicadas *cordon bleu*.

Rolling Boil
by Janna McMahan

"Never was a more unlikely pair." Grandma holds a stack of bright aluminum glasses in one hand, a pitcher clinking with sugary lemonade in the other. "How is it my two girls turned out so different?"

Momma and Aunt Lorena do look odd carrying the cooler. Momma takes two steps to my aunt's one. Lanky Aunt Lorena bends over to be even on her side. Momma checks her pies inside before they lift the cooler into the truck bed. She's like that, reminds you of a squirrel the way she's always picking at stuff. They make another trip and load up two boxes of icicle pickles in quart jars. Momma hoists herself up behind the steering wheel, cranks the engine and barely gives a glance back.

Grandma's housedress and apron are wet with sweat and flecked with yellow bits of corn. Small kernels are stuck in the soft gray curls that frame her droopy cheeks. Through the kitchen window I hear the pressure cooker jiggle and hiss.

"Well," Grandma says as she fills the shiny glasses. "Here we go again." She hands me one and the metal is cold on my fingers. The lemonade zings my tastebuds and makes my jaws ache.

"They'll probably be at one another fore they get out of sight," Pa says. He pulls a bandanna from his pocket and wipes his face and lips. A thin ridge of goo forms on his lower lip when it's hot outside.

Grandma settles down beside me on the tailgate and the shocks groan. I'm sandwiched in, a stick figure kid between two round grandparents. Pa uses a butcher knife to lop off the end of an ear of corn. Chickens scramble after the castoff. The truck bed behind us is filled past the cab window with green sweet corn waiting to be shucked.

"Mae, honey," Grandma says. "When they was your age your Pa there just about drove them two crazy playing tricks. He picked at them all the time. That's why they're how they are."

Pa grabs another ear, shucks, lops off the ends, drops it in a pan for me to silk.

"They're just high strung," he says and winks.

I grin too and start brushing silks to the ground. The strands make a shiny gold carpet below my feet. Some stick to my legs and itch.

"Hear 'em last week fussing over pickles?" Grandma says.

"Same thing every year," Pa says. "They stay at a rolling boil those two."

Grandma shakes her head. "Rena don't have the touch is all. She's just a pitiful cook, but Nola takes after me."

I share Aunt Lorena's kitchen failure. Momma tried to teach me to cook, but I never could get my fudge to soft ball or my angel biscuits to rise. I'm like Aunt Rena; neither of us has the touch. Still Aunt Rena keeps right on cooking even though she's been a widow woman since Korea.

Every church get-together or family homecoming people ask, "What did Lenola bring?" Momma never comes home with a crumb. She's asked to bake for every school bake sale because her cakes and pies always go for the most. People nearly fight over Momma's entries, but Aunt Lorena has her cooking passed over time and again. Once I saw Pa pay a boy to bid up Aunt Lorena's cookies.

I gulp my drink and head to wash up. The tub is cool against my bare skin and I swish the water so the Mr. Bubble will foam. Today is the Fourth and Momma expects me to look halfway decent. She always makes us clean up before going to town, even if it's just to the feed store. She says there's never been a body so poor they couldn't afford a bar of Ivory.

"Mae, you'd best not wear them flip-flops," Grandma says when I walk into the kitchen, rubber smacking my feet. I settle into her lap and her fingers divide my hair in a clean part from front to back. My head bobs and jerks as she wraps elastic bands around my hair and snaps the plastic balls over each other to secure my dog ears.

The stairs make a shriek like they plan to splinter with each step Pa takes down. He wears brown britches and a green short-sleeve shirt and carries his Sunday hat.

"Take your good shoes. You can change fore your momma sees you," he says.

Grandma kisses me and says, "Stay away from carnies. They don't know the Lord. They're gypsies." Grandma doesn't go with us. She never goes to town.

Nothing smells like the Fourth of July. The smoke from the 4-H chicken barbecue mixed with exhaust fumes from the parade. It's the same every year—ball players and cheerleaders on flatbeds, beauty queens waving from low-slung cars. The FFA drives tractors with flatbeds behind. Little leaguers ride the fire truck and hold their ears when the siren blasts. The school marching bands squeak and honk through the "Star Spangled Banner." Floats made from chicken wire and spray-painted newspaper wobble along the parade route. This year the Methodists have the winning float. Our church doesn't have a float because we're Baptist.

Later at the fair grounds Pa buys me sticky, pink cotton candy whirled around a paper cone. It reminds me of a hornet's nest. I ride the Ferris wheel while he watches. We flick dimes at a platter, but don't win. We wander over to the stockyard and inside a giant metal barn. There are rows and rows of livestock—sloe-eyed cows, tense horses, lots of sheep and pigs bumping around their stalls. There must be two dozen different kinds of chickens. I like the ones that are black and white polka dot and the ones with long shiny tail feathers that sweep out behind them.

After the awful manure of the barns it's easy to find the food tent. Inside it's quiet, the bawling cows and carnie barkers are distant. People here are waiting for the judges, holding their breath. The high school homeec teacher and Mayor Miller judge pies first. Momma's pie gets nudged out by a Holy-roller lady's peach and rhubarb cobbler. Momma would gripe that cobbler's not pie and should have its own category.

Canning is always last. Nearly anything can be canned so people get creative. Canning is judged on taste, smell and presentation. That's why Momma's careful to choose pickles all the same size and why she adds just a touch of green food coloring. The pickle division is the Kentucky Derby of the food fair, the Run for the Roses of cooking contests. Momma has eight blue ribbons hanging in the pantry at home. We all call it the trophy room.

Aunt Lorena made some icicle pickles this year too. It looks like too much trouble to me—two weeks of soaking and draining—first salt water, then alum. Then the pickling—vinegar, sugar and spices have to be poured over the pickles for days. On the fourth day the jars are sealed hot. The lids make a metal ting when they seal. It's my job to count the pops to make sure they all seal. Even when I tell Momma they all popped, she still runs her finger over the lids to check.

The judges crunch and smell and bend pickles and peer into jars. Momma and Aunt Lorena sit in the front row with all the other pickle ladies. The mayor clears his throat and announces third place. Everyone claps politely and the winner clutches her white ribbon. Then the home-ec teacher holds up the red ribbon and calls out second place. A woman from our church steps up. Now momma moves to the edge of her seat. She told me this was the best batch she'd ever made.

The mayor holds up the big blue ribbon, he pauses, then smiles down at Aunt Lorena and says, "Congratulations." Aunt Lorena yanks the ribbon out of his hand and waves it in the air. The mayor tries to calm her down so they can get her picture for the newspaper. Momma sits real straight in that folding chair. I can see her grinding her teeth.

Pa whistles and whispers, "Glad I ain't sleeping at your house tonight."

I look down at my flip-flops and pray.

A few days later we're killing and dressing chickens. Spring chicks are fat fryers now. Only the best laying hens and the mean old rooster avoid the freezer. Pa scatters feed and the dumb hens come running. He snags one's leg with his coat hanger hook, stretches her neck between two big nails in the tree stump and chop! Sometimes he'll have two or three headless chickens flopping around in the dirt. I usually go to the barn and play with the kittens while this goes on.

When the chickens stop flopping around Pa dunks them in a kettle of boiling water to loosen the feathers. Grandma picks off pinfeathers and Aunt Lorena burns brown paper bags to singe off hair. Momma pulls out the insides and plops them in a big wash pan. Dozens of soft, pale eggs about the size of shooting marbles come out too.

The smell alone is enough to keep me away, so usually they tease me while they work. "Get on over here, Mae, and learn how to clean chickens. You like fried chicken, don't you? You're gonna be hungry come winter."

But today nobody jokes or talks. Momma's stopped bellyaching about the pickle contest, but we're all still careful what we say. The only fun all day was when Pa sneaked up behind Grandma, grabbed her wrist, then grabbed the electric fence. The current made Grandma's hair stand on end and she squalled like he'd killed her.

Pa's shocked the living daylights out of all of us at one time or another. It's like a firecracker going off in your hand, like a million ants marching all over your body, especially your tongue. But none of us will grab the fence to return the favor.

So we're all pretty tight-lipped. Just every so often Aunt Rena will hum a happy little tune. Grandma and Aunt Rena go to the kitchen to put the last of the fryers in freezer bags. Momma and Pa clean up.

Shiny June bugs hum and bounce over the clover in our yard. I have a big one tied to a piece of thread and it flies this way and that. I let go of the string when I hear Momma say, "All I want is truth, Daddy."

"I swear," Pa says. "You think I'd do that?"

"I opened the jars. Mine tasted off, but Rena's tasted fine. Somebody switched the labels."

"That may be so, but it weren't my doing."

"You put the labels on this year. I asked you to do it myself."

Pa's quiet, and then he says, "Well, blame me if you want. Let's just keep peace."

This flies all over Momma. She grabs the last pan of guts and stomps across the barn lot headed for the creek.

Grandma comes out the back door with the egg basket on her arm. "What's she sulled up about now?" she asks.

"Thinks I switched the pickle labels."

"That so," Grandma says.

"Seems I recall you sent me out to the root cellar for something. Said you'd label the jars."

"Humph."

"Got anything to say for yourself, Ida?"

"It didn't hurt Rena none to win and it sure didn't hurt Nola to lose for once."

Pa ponders her words, then he says, "Reckon I'll go on letting her think I did it."

"That's right big of you," Grandma says. She takes my hand. "Honey, come help me gather eggs." On our way to the chicken house she says, "Mae, some things don't bear repeating. You understand?"

"Yes, ma'am."

"Good. Now, you go on in and start getting the eggs. I've got to visit the little house."

Inside the hen house, dust and hay drift through the air and tickle my nose. Some hens are cooing on the roosting pole, some are in their cubbyholes. I'm trying to get my hand under an old hen without getting pecked when I see something move on the other side of the dirt-smeared windows. Pa is sneaking along the backside of the outhouse where the electric wire runs from the barn to the hog lot. It's one of his favorite places to sock it to us. He looks like a peculiar toad crouched down with his hands on the ground in front of him, ready to jump at Grandma when she comes out.

Then I see Momma standing still at the side of the brooder house. She'd been rinsing out the pan at the spigot there, but now she's watching Pa and he's watching the outhouse door rattle that dry creaky way that says someone's finished their business.

Pa's ready to jump, but Momma beats him to it. She steps forward, throws the pan of water all over Pa and grabs hold of his ear. I saw the electricity arc toward Momma's fingers right before she grabbed the fence wire.

Pa yells, "Aarrgghh!" and kicks his feet up high in a jerky dance. Grandma screams, then says, "Oh, my Lord!" when she sees what has happened. The women laugh and laugh until they're wiping tears. Pa crawls to standing by leaning on the side of the outhouse. He starts walking around trying to shake the shock treatment and then he's laughing too. Their uproar bounces off the barn and echoes down the holler. Hogs squeal and run away. Chickens scatter. My cousins up on the ridge said they thought it was haints in the woods, but Grandma told them later that there's no such thing as haints, only the devil inside us all.

Pa never shocked any of us ever again. Grandma said he just needed a little lesson in "do unto others."

Grandma never told anyone that it was me put the wrong labels on the jars. She'd let me help and I just made an honest mistake like kids will do. She grinned when she saw what I'd done. She pressed a bubble out from under a label and smoothed it down flat.

"Don't worry about it," she said. "It don't matter at all."

Stew
by Ann Pelletier

1 Tbsp olive oil	Spill of sun from long ago. Stubby olive groves. Aromatic enticement. "Come in," you trill, but he is nowhere near this home.
1 lg onion, sliced	The sous chef does not cry. Defective lachrymal ducts? A hundred onions. Wild ones on mountain trails—Little Pete's Meadow where you thought you might sleep.
1 pepper, deseeded	Decapitate. Rinse away the flea egg seeds. The cat escaped the open window. Returned the night you gave up.
2 leeks	"Iron," said the man to the anemic victim. She had swooned into him. Or so he likes to tell it.
2 stalks celery	The inside prized, blonde-green. Pinch of salt brings out its bitter. *We laid down and wept for thee Zion.*
Handful mushrooms washed and sliced	Did they think you'd put them in this filthy? Red fungi, Point Lobos. And pines. And poison oak.
4 tomatoes, peeled and quartered	"If the skin goes, I go." False red from ethylene. Too young to be severed from the vine. Too little time a-bed. Abiding. Come back to me to ripen and to rot.
Kidney beans	Cat will come when I open the can. Full o' hope. I know, I know. I should think: crock pot; start dry and early; plan. If I could plan I'd have returned with him to Spain, spongy sun in orange groves.
Shake of paprika	His Hungarian past. Grandmother's photo taken by grandfather and his brownie camera. Rounded woman with bible, apron, hair swept back. He has not one memory.
	Pay attention. Cook gently. What was a heap collapses.

Three Poems
by Gaylord Brewer

The Black Pigs

They live days rooting fenced fields,
quiet, predestined days of grunt or squeal,
stiff-gallop after the afternoon train
then fall again to idleness or reflection.
In early evening, before the kestrel
arrives to commence its solitary rituals,

I amble over rail tracks to join them,
expound my theories on the dead and briefly
living. They are patient, practical pigs
and pass me in ragged file, a few twisting
magnificent stubbled snouts to scent
my arguments through rungs of fencing.

Soon enough, it is back to burrowing
dust and scraggy creekbed for whatever
unlikely insight might avail itself
until those last blessèd months of acorn
before the knife. Philosophy a pig can use.
For me, it is back for a hot scrub,

a secular sacrament. The cotton of bread
weighted with thin slices of my hosts,
striated, beautiful, darker than the wine,
trimmed neatly but not excessively

by the Saturday pork-monger who wishes
for me always a good week. The ribbon

of fat is thick and white, the brined flesh
an indulgent perfection. I lick fingers
clean of this wildly expensive grease
then ruin them for another bite,
teeth cutting easily the encasing crust,
rendering the meat delicately into strips.

I mouth the grape's blood, consider
my porcine brothers small in the distance.
When the hawk arrives from the west,
holding, fluttering, limned and hungry
against a fading bow of dusk, another day
is nearly lost forever, very nearly.

Apologia for Cooking

> *Here are grunions at their best.*
> —James Beard

For Monday birthdays, Italian in full regalia—
veal chops painted in pale butter, seared with grapes
and sherry vinegar; handmade pappardelle with parsley
from the garden, topped with international
envoy of fresh shitakes, baby 'bellos, and the star,
the flirt, irrepressible *boletus edulis*, or *funghi
porcini, prodotti tipici*, sautéed simply in diced shallot
and white wine, chardonnay admittedly, but
of unusual wit, finally pasta and 'shrooms perfumed
with black truffle virgin oil from the lips
of your coveted flask. To the side glass—left for you,
right for her—a 2000 Centine unassuming as old Tuscano

itself. Next day, after unfair dreams, you're back,
a quick walk, review of values and resolves
during a hot tub turn in bubbles, and onto Tuesday
anniversaries and French position—returned to the garden
to scissor thyme and rosemary from between stones,
rack of lamb massaged with Dijon mustard-bread jacket,
carré d'agneau à la moutarde, then that peasant
pleasure *haricots verts* but tumbled with wicked
flirtation of ginger before pairing of toasted almonds,
then: the showpiece: double-baked Yukon golds,
smashed with butter and cream and milled black pepper
and, again, liberal douse of truffle infusion
and spooned like babies into sturdier Idaho baker
skins—latter's flesh divided between bin and dog—
before topping of skillet-seared slices of foie gras,
shaved truffle, flowering drizzle of still more oil.
For libation you may ask modest forgiveness—not French,
but more-than-presentable 1997 Alexander Valley Zin
from Sausal's private reserve. It comports itself
in complex company. And now, places determined,
candles lit, your song low and luminous. Perhaps love's
on wing, perhaps October breezes blow just right.
Perhaps in any case the world's yours, time's now—
to extend a chair to your partner in life, to sit at last,
take a weight off, and stuff your storied guilt.

Apologia for a Frozen Surplus

The connective tissue, method to the madness, listen:
By day three we had carved the Holiday carcass to bone,
to shred and tendon. No one moved from the table.
Enough delicacy, I decided, gave Tate flannel to warm her,
hammered every style of homebrew down Saul's throat.
I couldn't stay still or shut my trap; my head danced.

Then, since Saul and I had discussed on the long
highway from Fiery Gizzard State Park, apropos of nothing
except to muzzle silence, his dislike of goat meat
and since by some bizarre serendipity I had recently
bought (with cash) several pounds of prime goat tenderloin
from the rear of a van in a deserted parking lot
from a man named Ruple I'd never met (1-917-TRY-GOAT),
this seemed the choice evening to fling wide the door
of my overweighted, top-loading freezer and reveal all.
My neatly taped brown-paper packages of goat, my stack
of rabbits, my quart of duck fat frozen pure as snow,
my bags of edamame (in and out of shell) and blackberries,
my bries en croûte, organic butter salted and unsalted,
spicy pesto, squid salad, tettnanger hops, leg of lamb
and three racks, handmade smoked salmon tortellini, etc.
I've been moody lately, distracted, eat nothing but
cold cuts, tomato soup, martinis. Even well lit in
the whispery glow of the open freezer door, cataloging my
dominance as hunter and gatherer, my mastery of technology
and international economic forces, I sometimes feel
queasy behind the pride, a twinge in the confidence.
But I stood before them anyway, glorified in my bounty,
one hand extended like a grinning starlet dangling
her *Price Is Right* grand showcase—the car, the cruise,
the new luggage, everything yours if you guess it right,
come closest to our cost without going over. Tate
was fighting for breath and Saul sat stiffly silent.
As I held the door and nodded, he never opened his mouth.

Pancakes

by Alexa Raine-Wright

"Ok, Robert. Mommy's sick today, so we have to make breakfast ourselves," ten-year-old Samantha says to her four-year-old brother on a warm, sunny, early-July morning. "What should we make?"

"Bloobry pancakes! Bloobry pancakes! Bloobry pancakes!" Robert replies, and starts dancing in a circle and clapping his hands ecstatically. He loves blueberry pancakes. So does Samantha, but she's never made them before.

"Well…ok." Blueberry pancakes shouldn't be too hard to make, she thinks. "Go ask Mommy if we can make pancakes," she says, as an afterthought. Robert runs out of the kitchen and into his mother's room. A minute later he runs back out, whispering, "She says yes, but we have to be very quiet, 'cause Mommy says she's going to sleep."

"Thanks," Samantha says, thumbing through the index of a cookbook. She likes to cook, and she's helped her mother make dinner several times. Robert likes to make food, too, but he usually proves to be more of a hindrance than a help. His chubby face peers excitedly over his sister's shoulder.

"Can I help? Can I help?" he asks.

"Yes, just a minute, Robert." Having found the recipe for blueberry pancakes, Samantha glances at the ingredients. "You go pick the blueberries, Robert." They have a blueberry bush in the garden. It has berries on it, but the children don't know that it's not blueberry season yet. The berries are still green. That's not a problem for Robert, who bounds outside, letting the screen door slam shut in his eagerness to help.

Robert picks a green berry and eats it, then he spits it out because of the sour taste. Thinking that putting them in the batter will make them sweet and purple, he gathers them in the bowl that he swiped from the kitchen counter.

Meanwhile, Samantha has begun the recipe. She puts the flour, sugar, baking powder, salt, and nutmeg together in a bowl. She had trouble finding the baking powder—she finally found it on a high shelf in the pantry after several cereal boxes had been knocked to the floor. Robert races inside with a bowl full of green blueberries.

"Those aren't going to work!" Samantha says, disappointed. "They're green!"

"But there aren't any blue ones," Robert tells her.

"Well, we'll see what else we have in the fridge."

"We can't use bloobries?"

Samantha doesn't answer him, but, after a minute of rummaging around in the fridge, pulls out a bag of cherries. She tosses her long brown hair over her shoulder in triumph. As Robert sees them, his face (which he had pulled into a pout) lights up. "Cherry pancakes!" he exclaims happily, and rather loudly.

"Shhh!" Samantha gives him a look and then sets up a stool for him to pit cherries. Though Samantha sets out two bowls (one for the cherries, one for the pits), Robert doesn't understand this. The pitted cherries and the pits go into one bowl and the stems go in the other.

Samantha whips the eggs (though not quite as thoroughly as they should be) and adds them to the milk. All is going quite well, she thinks, for her first time making pancakes. But she has forgotten to put the pan on the stove to get it hot.

Samantha drags a chair over to the stove and stands on it. Even though she is ten, she's still too short to reach the stovetop. She puts the pan on the burner, and turns the burner knob onto medium.

Then she mixes the dry and the wet ingredients together. Some of the flour makes clouds in the air, and Samantha accidentally inhales it. It tickles her throat and makes her cough. She finishes mixing what can now be properly called "the batter," and while she gets a drink of water she asks Robert to add the cherries. Her back is turned to him, so she doesn't see him add the cherries, and the pits, to the batter. He stirs them in and Samantha comes back and pours the batter into small puddles in the pan. She checks the cooking time—"Cook for two minutes, then flip carefully and cook for two minutes more," the cookbook says.

"Ok, Robert, we're going to count to sixty." They begin counting and Robert falls out after twenty. So he counts to twenty again. When Samantha has counted to sixty two times, she flips the pancakes. This is kind of hard, she thinks. The pancake is sticking to the pan, and the edges won't come up at all. The pancake breaks in half.

"Oops," Samantha says quietly. The other pancakes stick, too. She realizes that she forgot to put cooking spray on the pan.

She flips the pancakes more or less in their whole state, counts to sixty twice, scrapes them off the bottom, and slaps them on a plate.

"Pancake time?" Robert whispers hopefully, his eyes wide and plaintive.

"Get out two plates, two forks, two knives, and two napkins," replies Samantha, "and soon it'll be pancake time."

Samantha rummages in a cupboard for some cooking spray and sprays the pan thoroughly. She pours the batter on. This time, the pancakes lift easily from the bottom of the pan, and flip unbroken. She hears the noises of Robert collecting the table settings, and before she knows it, Samantha's used up all the batter and has made quite a lot of pancakes. A sense of pride makes her chest puff out.

She turns off the stove, picks up the plate of pancakes and carries it over to the table. Robert has put the table settings in a hodgepodge pile on one corner of the table. But he is nowhere in sight. Samantha sighs and sets the table herself. He has forgotten the knives, but remembered the maple syrup. There is also a cup full of water on the corner. Why not two cups? Samantha wonders. Just then she hears the screen door slam and Robert races into the kitchen, clutching a fistful of dandelions and daisies. He sticks them in the cup of water and smiles.

They finally sit down to eat. Robert grabs the maple syrup and dribbles it all over his pancakes. Samantha does, too.

Samantha's first bite of pancake contains something very hard—it doesn't break when she chews, either. She keeps it under her tongue and spits it out once she's chewed the rest of her bite (which is delicious). It's a cherry pit. She thinks it's an accidental pit, but her next bite has one too. She guesses what has happened but only warns, "Watch out for the cherry pits, Robert."

He nods, his mouth full of cherry pancakes, syrup covering his chin. A small pile of pits sits on the tablecloth beside his plate.

Not bad for a first batch of pancakes, Samantha thinks.

Not bad at all.

Interview with Mark Kurlansky

Writer Mark Kurlansky has an insatiable curiosity and the research enthusiasm of a Sherlock Holmes. He's produced a veritable library of books spanning historical, political, and social subjects, plus outstanding fiction, and within it all quite a lot about food. His New York Times best-selling books Cod: A Biography of the Fish That Changed the World, and Salt: A World History have given readers a whole new way to view our historical context—through what we eat. His latest novel Boogaloo on Second Avenue is a smorgasbord of love, murder, and eating through the multicultural culinary world of New York's Lower East Side. Still to come—among other books—is a fiction collection, Edible Stories, and The Big Oyster: New York on the Half Shell. Alimentum had a revealing conversation with Mark from his current locale for research—Gloucester, Massachusetts.

It's interesting how *Salt* and *Cod*, by delving into the history of these foods, map out a social and political history as well.

Food is a great marker for history and culture. It's a little frustrating, though, when I read historical accounts, I'm always frustrated that they don't tell you more about what people were eating. I wish diaries were full of meals, and sometimes they are. But I wish there were a lot more. Food just tells you a lot. I'm spending the summer in Gloucester. And if you look at the food and people here, I mean, first of all: chowder. You have the whole New England evolution of chowder. I'm in a town where people eat fish and clam chowder and…cannelloni, because half, literally half of the fishermen, are Sicilian.

Would you find chowder in Sicily?

You'll find a kind of chowder anywhere there are fishermen. The ingredients of the chowder tell you everything about the fishery. New Englanders used to eat cod chowder and now eat clam chowder.

The three books *Cod*, *Salt*, and *The Basque History of the World* seem interconnected. Did research for one lead to another?

Cod came first and *Basque* is a subject that I was interested in long before *Cod*. I always thought that I would love to do a book on the Basque, but who would be interested? And people were so intrigued by the Basque parts of *Cod*, it's what reviewers and readers singled out when I gave talks. And the publisher, George Gibson at Walker, asked me if I'd be interested in doing something on the Basques, which, you know, I'd been waiting for thirty years for somebody to ask.

And *Salt* came directly out of *Cod*. I mean, I started thinking about the historic role of salt because of its role in the fisheries. I mean the main role of geologists, just like today, is to find oil and other minerals. The main role of geologists always had been to find salt and understand how it was made and where to find it. But they didn't really have a lot of technology for drilling and for understanding what was under the surface of the earth. So they had no idea. They knew the oceans were full of salt, but it wasn't profitable to make sea salt unless you were in a sunny climate.

Why is food such an attractive subject for you?

Because it's so personal, and yet has such broad implications. You know, it really reflects so much about history and yet it's this basic thing that everybody does. It's a universal experience. And everybody loves it. I don't believe people who say they don't care about food. It's like people saying they don't care about sex. They're repressing something.

It's interesting how food and sex often intertwine in writing.

They're the two great subjects for writers, because they're so personal and so universal. And because they're about sensory experiences, they're very challenging to write well about.

Tell us about how food finds its way into fiction for you. And how does that contrast with writing about food in nonfiction?

It's very similar in a way, except that you're kind of making it up. But you're not making up the food. I mean, to me, if you create characters, they will—by virtue of who they are and where they come from—they will eat certain kinds of food and it will be incorporated into their lives. And so it's a great way of developing characters.

Do you give characters your own personal connections to food?

It depends on who they are. If they're Sicilian or if they're Jewish…people use food to kind of express who they are, to express their economic class and sometimes express their roots. Like affluent Jewish people eat *shtetl* food on Jewish holidays, but don't touch it the rest of the year. Or in my book, in *Boogaloo*, this family eats this stuff every Friday night, even though they don't even like it.

It's interesting to eat food you don't like if you don't have to.

Because it's your roots. I've known Italian people who have talked about how they hate pasta. They hate pasta because it's all they got when they were kids. You go back to it sometimes though, because it's who you are. It's remembering your family.

How would you describe the history of your palate?

Well, I was raised in New England and I was always very drawn to seafood. And I spent a lot of my life in Europe, mainly living in Paris. So I suppose there's a French influence. Or Spain. I spent a lot of time in Spain.

Did those cuisines change the way you thought about food?

Yes. I mean, the markets did. It took me years to understand all these things are just underdevelopment. I mean that New York had markets like Les Halles. But they're all closed down now.

Was Les Halles there when you were in Paris?

It had just closed. But still the neighborhood markets were very good. I've had a lot of different influences. I used to be a pastry maker and was very influenced by Central European pastry. Hungarian and Austrian and German. And I think that's because they're the kind of desserts that my grandmother used to make. My grandmother used to make the most wonderful strudel.

You've focused on strudel in your book *Boogaloo on Second Avenue*.

Yes, but in a very ungrandmotherly way.

You include recipes in many of your books. How do they fit into your narratives?

I think recipes are great artifacts. And they don't have to be good. They just have to be written in an interesting way or be interesting in reading. In my *Cod* book a lot of those recipes are horrible, but they're interesting.

When you read a recipe can you almost taste it…know what it's going to be like?

Usually. Sometimes old recipes, 17th century and earlier, are a little hard to figure out because they have unwritten cultural references that we don't know or have to look up. But, yes, I can generally look at a recipe pretty quickly. But the recipes in *Boogaloo on Second Avenue* are something kind of different. They're written in the voices of the characters. I thought it would be fun as a further expression of the characters to have them tell recipes.

Did their recipes help reveal character for you?

It's in their voices. I mean if it's one Sicilian guy giving a recipe and he says things like use Italian olive oil, don't use that French stuff or it will be awful. And up here in Gloucester I was getting a recipe from a Sicilian guy for something else I'm working on. And he used almost the same words about parsley. He said—and this is a year after I finished the book—he said use Italian parsley, don't use that awful little wrinkly stuff.

You're working on a few books at once. There's the oyster book due out next spring, and the fiction collection *Edible Stories*. Can you tell us about that?

It's a collection of short stories. Some of the same characters pop up in different stories, but not all of them. But what the stories all have in common is they're about people's relationships with food. I like writing short stories a lot. I write them regularly.

In this issue of Alimentum we're publishing a story from that collection called

"The Soup," in which a Native American is the last surviving speaker of her language.

I got the idea for that story because I actually met somebody in Alaska who had been a native speaker of her language. And she told me that an anthropologist used to visit her to learn the language, so I just sort of imagined what that would be like. I also have a book coming up called *America Eats*.

Isn't *America Eats* the name of a Nelson Algren book?

Well, the WPA had a project in the 1930's called America Eats, in which they asked all the out-of-work writers to do research in their region. It was broken up into regions—about what people were eating and the ways they were eating. It was very socially-minded. And Nelson Algren was one of them. So were Saul Bellow and Zora Neale Hurston. And the whole thing was never published. So somebody separately published Nelson Algren's contribution. But the whole thing was packed into boxes and sits in those boxes in the Library of Congress. When World War II broke out and the WPA ended, it was never done.

And you're going to edit it?

So I'm going to do it. It was never put together. I mean, you couldn't possibly do it all, but I'm going to try to pick the best stuff. It was all in regions. The New York part of it is just a mountain of stuff. And I'm not sure if that stuff is duplicated in the Library of Congress or not or if there's stuff still lying out in other regions. I'm going through it and trying to pick the best and writing introductions. And I may go back to some of these places and see how it's changed, because a lot of the writing is about traditional gatherings.

What a great document of the country.

Yes, it was intended to be. But the WPA had all these great ideas. And it wasn't done in a dumb sort of way. I mean it took on issues of race and all kinds of things.

Do you have any favorite food literature you'd like to mention?

There's another thing I'm doing. I'm translating a Zola novel. It's a wonderful novel that takes place in the 1840's in the Les Halles market, and is all about food as metaphors for society and politics. The book begins with an emaciated guy who's escaped from the French Guyana penal colony. And he's making his way back to Paris and he's almost there but collapses in the middle of the road. And suddenly he hears a voice shout: *get out of the way! the wagons are coming!* And somebody hoists him up and throws him to the side of the road and all these wagons full of food headed for Les Halles come by and somebody gives him a ride. And he's just sick because he's starving and he's on this wagon full of food, but he can't eat it. The whole book is like that.

What other food literature do you like?

It seems that great food cultures produce great food literature. There are wonderful Chinese stories and novels that have a lot about food in them. There's a great novella called *The Gourmet* by a writer named Lu Wenfu. It's wonderful. And the Italians to a certain degree also. That Sicilian book, *The Leopard*, has great food descriptions in it. It's interesting the cultures that have food in their literature. Most writers at some point or another write about food, but some obviously do it better than others. The French novelists do great food descriptions. Zola was great on food. So was Balzac.

You've got so many books going at once. What's your work schedule like?

I work every day—ten, twelve hours a day.

Is some of that editing time?

Depending on what I'm working on.

Does writing about food make you hungry?

No. It's not so much about the food. It will often make me nostalgic for places or experiences rather than the food itself.

Do you eat while you write? When it's time to have something to eat, do you just bring it over to your computer?

I do. I do, but I try not to eat much. I'm afraid...

What do you mean?

Trying to lose weight.

But you must enjoy food, right?
I do.

What's a favorite food of yours?
Well, I really like seafood. I like good, fresh out of the water, whole grilled fish. That's about the best thing I can think of.

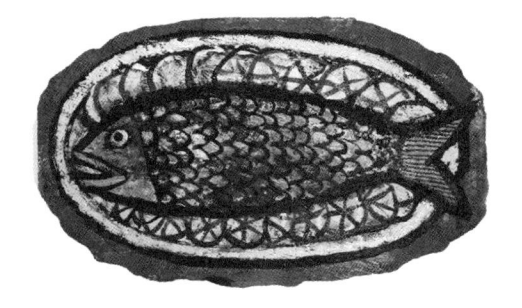

The Soup
by Mark Kurlansky

Mrs. Janie Powell Joseph peered deep into the steamy stock pot with approval and put the lid back on, slightly ajar to let just a little steam escape—warm fish-laden puffs to fill her trailer. The dish was known in her language as "The Soup." In her language she was called "Light Before Dawn." But no one called her that anymore because no one spoke her language.

She looked through the small window of her aluminum trailer out onto the flat land—miles of it with summer grasses, the truest green she knew and summer flowers giving little flecks of color. She could see past the one-story houses of Anchorage to the berry-stain-purple mountains. And that was as far as she could see. One day the roofs would go all the way to the mountains. She felt a shudder run through her and she went back to the stove to stir The Soup again, as though she needed the steam for its heat.

Then back to the window, to the berry-stained mountains, the purple wall on her horizon, beyond which she could not see. She knew what was there. The black sea and the blue lake, Lake Kish'da y'k, the Lake of The People, and above it rising like a god's frightening love, the white crowned dark face of Mount Kish'da y'k, the Mountain of The People, her far away home, just a few enormous crests of Alaska away.

From EDIBLE STORIES
by Mark Kurlansky
Copyright © 2008 by Mark Kurlansky
Published by arrangement with Ballantine Books,
an imprint of Random House Publishing Group, a division of Random House, Inc.

Back to The Soup, the flavor of the steam feeding her through the pores of her skin. It always made her remember Salmon Lady who fed her The Soup, and later taught her to make it and how she made it for Rocky Coast and how he loved it and how she loved him. All gone, now there was only she, Janie Powell Joseph in Anchorage and there was still The Soup.

The telephone rang. She knew no one any more. They were all gone. They didn't use telephones anyway. But it came with the trailer she was bought when her land was sold. And she liked the telephone, the possibility that someone would call.

"Heller? Mrs. Janie Powell Joseph. Are how you afternoon?"

It was that professor. They had a bargain. She was the last to speak her language. The last native speaker of the Kish'da y'k people left behind on earth. For what purpose she had been left behind she did not yet know.

He wanted to learn her language and speaking to her was his only way to learn. She spoke with him to speak with someone. To speak again in The Language. So she told him that she was home making fish soup and if he wanted to he could come over.

"Thank it so much Mrs. Joseph. I be there in a right off."

"Yes, yes, yes," she said, hanging up the phone and stirring The Soup. Soon she heard a hollow tapping on the aluminum door and an intruding voice that slapped the air, flat as the smack of a beaver tail, "Mrs. Powell! Are it I, Dr. Krauss."

She gave a last stir to The Soup and closed the lid on the pot, like tucking a child in safely before opening the door. "Hello, leader Krauss," she greeted him in The Language, which had no word for doctor. "So good of you to come by."

"Oh not necessarily. Happily to see one, and spoke The Language of The People."

"Yes," she said. "It feels very good to speak The Language."

"MMM," he said. "Smells it so good here. What cook you?"

"Oh, it's just something The People make." She looked a little embarassed. "It's a fish soup. The People always make it. Especially in the late summer when the salmon spawn and float." She stopped a brief second to appreciate nature's idea of spawning and then dying. Would it be better to die when your purpose had been served?

"The white people don't like the spawned salmon. But the bears eat them and

The People make this soup."

"What called it?" Dr. Krauss asked, his pen cocked and notebook unfurled.

"We call it The Soup. Or we did. It's a fish soup."

Dr. Krauss wrote down the name and studied it on the page and then said in English, "Why that means 'the soup.'"

"Yes," she continued in The Language, "The Soup. It's a fish soup. Salmon. I would invite you to stay but white people never like it."

"Then you no one have share with it?" he said, returning to The Language.

"Not many," she said with a sad little smile. "There are a few of The People left. Half and half people like the old story of the woman who married the dog."

It was a story many Alaskan people told and Krauss just nodded. He knew the story. "And the half people speak not The Language?"

She smiled because she was too polite to laugh. "You speak The Language better than half people. They go to white school and forget everything."

"And your son?"

"He is not a half people," she said defensively.

"No," he quickly agreed. "I can suppose that. Some doubt the last of The People he, I to guess."

"Yes," she said. "I suppose he is the last. But really I am the last because he can't speak The Language. Those who do not speak the language of The People are not truly The People. You study these things. Wouldn't you say that's true?"

"I think will I, yes."

She looked out the aluminum square of window at the berry-stained mountains that she could not see beyond. Even now they had white on top that ran down in streaks like melting whipped cream. But the sun was still high in the sky and warm and bright. "When he was very young his name was Trees Standing Together and he spoke The Language. But it was about that time that all the leaders decided to give up their land and become a company like the white people. And because we were doing this it was thought to send all our children to white schools and Trees Standing Together became Bob." She chuckled a little to herself, still looking out the window. "Bob. And Bob cannot remember The Language. He bought me this 'trailer.'" There is no word for trailer in Kish'da y'k so she said it in English.

"His wife is from the Tlingit people down the coast. She speaks her language and he has learned a little. But I don't understand a word of it and their children will only speak English." She put her hands to her face and tugged as though her features were a hairpiece she was straightening. Then she picked up her long-handled wooden spoon, lifted the lid off the pot and stirred a little.

"This a good to smell!" Dr. Krauss said cheerfully.

"He bought me this 'trailer,'" she said. Then she giggled wickedly to herself, "I can't blame him. Who could he marry? His generation only had one girl. Six boys and one girl. I suppose one of them married her—Eaglefish. That's what she looked like. A nose like an eagle and two beady little eyes. Better to marry a Tlingit. Where did the other boys go?" she suddenly asked as though she had never thought of this before. "They couldn't speak The Language either but I could make them The Soup. That would be good."

Dr. Krauss looked at her with sympathy. "Does Bob shout at you?"

She looked at him quizzically and so he tried again.

"Does he cry out to you?" Then he pointed at the telephone.

"Oh," she understood. "Call, we say. Does he call me? We are not ones for the telephone. He writes me. He and his wife have moved south to the lower states. He writes me. He writes."

"And who is he doing?" Dr. Krauss asked.

"Oh, he's fine," she answered and then thought better of her answer. "We don't have a language to write each other in. He can only write in English."

"And you can not English to read?"

She stared at him stubbornly. Then she got up and stirred her pot. "I can read it. But it is very slow. I once read a letter of his and it took three days' work. So I just answer him in English about how the seasons are changing. The snow coming and going and the salmon arriving and the bears coming down to fish them. And I thank him for the trailer. What else can you say in English?"

"Where the letters to be found. I can help them to read you and then we can answer it together!"

She eyed him inch by inch, the way you eye a dog to decide whether it is dangerous. This was too much. What did this leader, this 'doctor,' want? She could let him practice The Language, though she was not clear on why he wanted to learn a language that nobody spoke, that was leaving no written word behind, that would soon vanish when she did. But she would not let him into her letters. That was too much. "Well," she said tapping her thighs, "I would ask you to stay, but white people really don't like The Soup."

"Oh, but like I all things. I can to try?"

He stood up and she took her post by the soup as though to protect it from assault. "It is a fish soup but white people never like it."

"But you know how interest I be in all being from The People," he pleaded.

"Well, come see," she agreed with a friendly beckoning gesture and removed the lid from the pot while gently moving the soup with her wooden spoon. He looked in and to his surprise the soup looked back up at him. In the milky churning broth were dozens of eyes, blind little eyes staring blankly, for they were cooked and cloudy. Salmon eyes seemed to drift around the broth in confusion and roll over trying to look up the way blind eyes do sometimes, seeking out light.

Dr. Krauss knew that he could not eat The Soup, could not eat salmon eye soup and she had known that all along so there was no need for anything more to be said about it. They exchanged warm goodbyes and he promised to "Come be on top of you again" and she thanked him and he left.

She went back to the stove and lifted the wooden spoon to her mouth and sipped. It was ready. It tasted of her memory of Salmon Lady so many years ago and Rocky Coast who she missed, and sitting by the Lake of the People talking of things while skinning tough-hided animals. She opened a drawer and took out a stack of letters and ran her thumb along the edges. Most had not been opened. She placed them carefully on her table and ladled a bowl of The Soup and placed it on the table next to the letters. She looked out the window one last time because, strangely, in a trailer you could not look at the outdoors and sit and eat at the same time. The window was too high.

She looked out the window. The sun was still very high. No darkness would fall this week. These were the long bright nights when they used to sit by The Lake and eat The Soup.

In the Soup
from A Paris Notebook
by Andrew Daubigny

"Alaine—he makes zee best soups," Rolande had told me. "Wait until you taste one of them. Zey are zee best soups in ze world."

Rolande, an international lawyer, had invited me to live as artist-in-residence in the village of Bozouls, Aveyron, in the southwestern corner of France, an area rugged with mountains and gorges. Hugging both basin and rim of an eight-hundred foot gorge, the tiny village of Bouzols featured two medieval stone sentry towers, attached to one of which was an efficiency apartment equipped with a Jacuzzi.

This would be my home and my studio for three weeks.

As things worked out, I never saw my hostess, who got tangled up in a complex case back in New York City. Except for the caretaker, Alaine, and Mama Maguy, Rolande's eighty-nine-year-old mother, who lived high up in the tower itself, I was left entirely on my own.

After picking me up from the train station, Alaine (who, with his long stringy black hair and pointy chin—augmented by a pointier goatee—reminded me of d'Artagnan in *The Three Musketeers*) let it be known that I was to join him and Mama Maguy for a dinner of soup one evening. *"T'en fait pas, t'en fait pas,"* he promised, and promptly disappeared.

Which suited me fine. I had my own door, and my own key, and having come from New York I welcomed some privacy. I painted in the mornings, and wrote before and after dinner at one of the cafes at the top of the gorge. I'd write till ten or eleven p.m., then return to my lodgings where I'd taped my paintings to my room's craggy stone walls (the entire village was made of stone). I would have liked to lie naked in the Jacuzzi looking up at the stars before bed, but the Jacuzzi didn't work.

As for Mama Maguy, the way she'd been described to me I had an image of a fabulous withered old Wizard of a woman presiding over the town and all its doings from her cloudy perch. Everyone in Bouzouls knew her, or knew of her; when I'd mention her name faces would light up and eyes would smile. *"Ah, oui, Mama Maguy!"* they'd say, and launch into an anecdote that in short order would have them either rolling with laughter or wiping tears from their eyes, or both. She was, apparently, the life of an ongoing party to which I'd yet to be invited.

I could not wait to glimpse this phenomenon myself, and tried a few times. But each time I knocked on the heavy oak door at the foot of the tower I got no answer. Instead, I heard what sounded like a large dog barking somewhere inside, the sound reverberating fiercely off the tower's sweaty stone walls. High above me, around the top of Mama Maguy's dizzying turret, a flock of white pigeons—or were they doves? —flapped their wings in the air. That was all.

Days passed. I spent them climbing up and down the walk from the bottom of the gorge to the top, where two cafes perched, the owners at war with each other. Although Rolande had warned me to choose one, the diplomat in me chose instead to divide my patronage between both establishments, inviting the scorn of each. At first I shrugged it off; I was an artist, after all, I told myself, and accustomed to indifference and hostility. I ate my *salade nicoises* and *croque monsieurs* and kept my own council.

But as the gruelingly humid summer days dragged by and my work proceeded less than gloriously, I grew more and more eager for company, and wistful, wondering: would I ever get to taste Alaine's famous soup?

At last, one afternoon, I ran into Alaine at one of the cafes.

"Ah, An-droo! An-droo!" (Alaine spoke in a thick patois and said everything twice.) "Tonight you must come to Mama Maguy's for soup! I make the very best soup! *A ce soir! A ce soir!*" he said, and hurried off.

Soup—by then it was a magic word! After twelve days of uninspired salads and sandwiches served to me by snarling cafe owners I was starved for some human warmth and for some authentic, homemade food!

Having barely finished a painting I was late for my 7 p.m. dinner invitation.

This time, when I knocked on the door, no dog barked. Instead I heard a voice and looked up and saw Alaine's pointed chin and stringy black hair dangling from a small window high above.

"*Moment!*" he yelled down at me.

Soon I was let in and led up the winding stairs to the top of the turret, where I arrived to find Mama Maguy and a young girl with blond hair seated at a large, heavy oak table. The young girl was Mama Maguy's housekeeper—one of several, apparently. As for Mama Maguy, she looked every one of her octogenarian years, and not at all like the feisty, perpetual instigator of mirth and tears I had come to expect. She wore a red and white striped blouse—the kind pizza chefs wear— that accentuated the parchment-like whiteness of her skin, and thin hair the color of straw. Her eyes were large and round and looked even larger and more myopic under the thick glasses that she wore. A bubble of drool clung to the edge of her lower lip. She sat at one end of the big table, while Magalie, her housekeeper, sat at the other, both with napkins tucked into their necks, waiting. On the table two candles burned.

And there, in its center, surrounded by a bottle of red wine, a bowl of grated cheese, and a cutting board with some bronze, crusty bread sliced into small cubes, was a large steel pot with a spoon poking out from under its lid. This, I calculated, was the famous pot of soup for which I had been invited, and whose heady, mushroomy smell filled the room.

"Ah, An-droo, An-droo," said Alaine, wagging a bony, sharp and warty finger at me as I took my seat—warning me, I supposed, that I was in for an unprecedented experience, though the gesture was more castigating than anything.

Beyond the window I heard pigeons—or were they doves?—flapping and cooing. I turned to Mama Maguy, who'd been Sphinx-like all this time, and said something in French to let her know I spoke the language, but she made no reply. Magalie was equally silent, her eyes lowered under sad bangs. I wondered if perhaps ritual required that no one speak until the meal was served, and the wine glasses were full, and grace had been said. As we sat there Alaine slowly, meticulously, ladled the soup, which looked dismayingly like porridge, into our wooden bowls. The savory mushroom smell grew dizzyingly strong. Wineglasses were filled. Alaine gave thanks to the Lord, and raised his glass in a toast to me and my successful residency.

Then, just as I was about to reach for my soup spoon, Alaine stood and announced that he had to make a phone call. He took a cell phone from the back pocket of his jeans and dialed. For the next forty or so minutes he marched around the table's perimeter, talking in a rapid, sing-song voice. Several times I filled my soup spoon and brought it close to my lips, only to see the others sitting there with their hands tucked in their laps as though in prayer, waiting. My French being adequate at best, I struggled to make out every other word of Alaine's phone conversation, wondering what could be important enough to deprive us all of our meals? From what I could gather topics discussed included—but were not limited to—the Algerian dilemma, Protestantism vs. Catholic tyrannies, and why wood had eclipsed coal as the fuel of choice in French villages. To whomever he had telephoned Alaine held forth that Amsterdam was a terrible place, and that drugs in general were evil, and that contrary to recent scientific studies depression was not genetic, and he could prove it, since three—three!—of his cousins (first cousins, by the way) had attempted suicide, one successfully, while he himself had never, ever in his life been the least bit depressed, not the least bit! Furthermore, he refused on principle to drink *Eau de Vie* or *Aquavite* ("*Il sont les boissons du diable!*"—"They are the devil's drinks!") declaring that wine was the strongest spirit a person should imbibe. "And did you know" (he told whoever he'd called) "that during the Second World War the corpses of over a dozen fetuses were discovered by soldiers in a wine cask in the woods behind the local abbey? It's true, it's true (*C'est vrai, c'est vrai!*)..."

I looked at my watch. We'd been sitting there for twenty minutes. I hadn't eaten since breakfast. Another fifteen minutes passed with Alaine still on the phone and the soup cooling and congealing in our bowls. He went on endlessly, throwing us a nod of his d'Artagnan chin every now and then, indicating that we should proceed without him, which I would have been glad to do had the others not sat there with their hands folded patiently in their laps. Mama Maguy seemed used to this scenario, as if it were part of the dinner ritual. By then she had fallen into a dreamy state, her frail fingers clasping the stem of her wine glass; she seemed to leave the room entirely, drifting on a cloud of white doves (or pigeons) to some Elysian sentry tower in the sky. Meanwhile Alaine discussed the hazards of fluoridation, the number of deaths each year from malaria, global warming, the expanding/contracting universe debate. I broke down and took a sip of my wine, catching Magalie's sorrowful look, a look that said *I go through this charade every night.* Alaine spoke on. Politics, philosophy, stem cell research..."*Bien sur, bien sur; peut-être, peut-être...*" I was sure we'd never taste our soups.

Then, just when I was about to abandon all hope, he put the phone away. "*Alors,*" he said, and had just tucked in his own chair when a voice rang up from outside. "Ah—*moment,*" he said, untucking himself, rising and going to the window, out of which he stuck his head to start another long conversation as our soups continued their alchemical journeys toward clammy mush.

To escape the sight of my solidifying soup I excused myself and went to the bathroom. There, where the odor of mushrooms had yet to penetrate, I smelled instead the old smell of invalids, the redolence of leaky catheter that is the smell of old Europe. Still I was glad to be safe in that bathroom and momentarily free of Alaine's *moulin a paroles* (windmill of words) and Magalie's pathetic frown and the terrible sound that Mama Maguy made with her supposedly real teeth, a scraping noise like Captain Queeg's steel balls being rubbed together, a sound that made me want to squeeze my eyes shut and think of places far, far away. When I could no longer justify staying in the bathroom I returned, only to find Alaine deep into his *flux de bouche,* with no end in sight, and Magalie still frowning and Mama Maguy grinding her teeth louder than ever.

Finally, saying "*Á demain! Á demain!*" Alaine waved off his invisible audience and returned to the table, looking shocked to see that we hadn't started without him. He said grace again.

Now, at last, I would get to taste the soup. I lifted up my spoon. But before I could taste a drop I had to hear how it was made, how Alaine had gone to a dozen markets in search of the very finest ingredients at their height of freshness: mushrooms, carrots, onions and leeks, how he'd chopped, diced, sauteed and sliced, making his own stock from veal and chicken bones, which he simmered, stirring in butter and salt, folding in cream for what sounded like hours, days, weeks.

And that was only the beginning, for as Alaine expounded at great length, the secret to a good soup was not in its original creation, but in its evolution, its accumulating character, like wine and people, over time—its journey from meal to meal, with enhancements and augmentations along the way, for the chopping and dicing of which he spoke had happened ages ago, and the soup that (with any luck) we were about to savor was in fact dozens of prior soups, historical soups, melded and grafted and simmered into one another over time—a soup of soups, with the original Ur-soup presumably dating back to the origins of organic life, to the amino-acid soup of creation itself. *"Bon appetit!"* said Alaine, toasting.

We ate.

Though lukewarm, it was a good, thick, salty soup, grayish-brown in color—the color of the stones of Bozouls—chowder-like in consistency. Still, I questioned Alaine's dicing and slicing. Those tiny bits of vegetable suspended in gray glop looked vaguely dehydrated, and were more than a little reminiscent of the ingredients in a Knorr Swiss pouch. And there was that unmistakable essence of MSG-fortified bouillon cube.

And then Mama Maguy, who'd been silent as a totem pole all this time, spoke up, and kept speaking, as if she were an internet site that had taken all this time to download. She loved Paris in the Fall, she said, and drank only Bordeaux in Summer, and loved her home, and herself. "Look at my stone walls," she said. "Look at my thick beams, look at my straight nose and my still blonde hair and my spanking white pigeons. Damned if I'm not the talk of this town! They say that my daughter, Rolande, is the talk of the town, but it's not true—*I* am the talk of the town. I *always was* the talk of the town. Look at me, don't I still look good? Under this eighty-nine-year-old flesh there is the body of a raving beauty. Oh, I was beautiful—more beautiful than Rolande! You know, I almost gave her up, and probably should have, the little wench! But I didn't; I stuck it out. No orphanage for my daughter. She worships me now, and why shouldn't she? I saved her life! If not for me, God knows—imagine what a different life she would have had—possibly no life *at all*—had I given her up as I had every right to do! We were so poor, you cannot imagine. Poverty—the worst disease of all! Every three months we had to pack up and move to cheat the landlord, always farther and farther away from the center of the city, my beloved Paris. Once I even made Rolande leave behind her doll collection in order to fool the *patron* into thinking we were coming back. Oh, she cried tears as salty as this soup (I think, Alaine, that you may have put too much salt in it this time)—but it beat the alternative, wouldn't you say? And do you think she was grateful? Of *course* she was! And then I even found her a father, a respectable man who gave her a last name. Yes, that's right: gaze upon me and my works in awe and wonder, here in my tower with my caretaker, my maidservant, my white doves that are really pigeons and my squeaky teeth!" Cold soup dribbled from her chin onto the napkin she wore tucked into her striped pizza blouse.

In addition to her occasional sly farts Mama Maguy gave off a faint but pungent odor of fermentation as some old people will, a tangy smell closely related to the smell in the bathroom and which invested itself into every spoonful of soup and sip of Bordeaux, making me gag slightly as I ate, watching her talk with her soupspoon dripping onto the cuff of her red striped sleeve, her globe-like eyes darting back and forth, back and forth under the milk-bottle lenses.

Meanwhile Alaine had gotten back on his cell phone again to continue the conversation of before, his wisp-thin lips moving at the speed of sound under his d'Artagnan mustache, his s's sibilating through the gap in his front teeth, his warty hand stirring the by now ice-cold soup. He spoke of genetic modifications to aubergines and other nightshades, of riots in Nepal, the need for earthquake-proof construction in third-world nations, of the threats being posed to the sovereignty of the Euro…He pronounced on fortified wines and cloning and improved techniques of spinal surgery…all the while stirring his prize soup, his Soup of Ages, his Infinite Soup, an alchemist wizard in his medieval tower-laboratory. And just as Alaine's soup was made mainly of past soups, and people's bodies are made nominally of water, Alaine's life, I realized, consisted mainly of words, a simmering cauldron of homemade, sliced, diced, constantly reconstituted words, salted with *"Peut-êtres"* and *"Bien surs,"* bubbling endlessly, served up night after night after night, grown cold in their bowls…

"Bien sur, bien sur! Sans doute, sans doute! Certainement! Certainement! Peut-être! Peut-être! And by the way, are you aware that it was a Frenchman who invented the so-called 'whirlpool bath'? However—as with so many other French inventions—the man, being a total nincompoop, neglected to apply for his patent on time, and therefore—)…

Italian Cuisine
by Paul Hostovsky

I'm visiting my half-sister Olga
in Bologna. She's 45 and married
to an Italian. I'm 15, American, and the only
Italian word I know besides spaghetti

is baloney. My family
history reads like one of those librettos
where everyone is falling in love and jumping
out of windows. Alleluia, allioop!

My nephew Dario, 4 years older than me (go
figure), takes me to a party on the Via Faenza
where everyone is smoking and eating Italian
pot brownies. They all take turns

practicing their English on the American.
I feel famous, then exploited.
Someone starts telling a long hilarious joke
in Italian. All of my interpreters

are cracking up and rolling on the floor
mute with laughter. I smile helplessly,
sweep the floor with my eyes for the dropped
English. It evaporates like water in a pot

of giddy spaghetti. The brownies kick in.
I float to the window, look out at the porticos leapfrogging

to infinity through the streets of Bologna.
I close my eyes and see

Olga in her kitchen, holding a rolling pin,
my father in Prague holding a cigarette
like a leaky pen, pointing it drippingly up
at a portrait of Jan Masaryk who

jumped (go figure) out a window.
I see Wendy Iazzoni back in Jersey
standing at the end of a tunnel in space—
I can see the gap between her teeth perfectly;

I can see the gap between the buttons
of her blouse, which was always space enough—
when Dario taps my scapula and we lapse
into English. Back at Olga's

it's rigatoni for dinner—
little fluted tunnels floating
in a white wine sauce. I'm still
stoned. I hold one drippingly up

to my left eye while closing
my right: Olga floats into focus
glaring like the Inquisition at Dario
who's holding a rigatoni telescope

of his own, peering through it across
the table at me, the American
Galileo. "Nevertheless,
it moves," I say, and we explode

into exorbitant laughter.

Ode to Risotto
by Donald Newlove

We were taken to the Gotham Restaurant tonight and I had duck and turnip risotto among the fancy folk and sophisticates. Hard to believe that a few turnip cubes and rich slices of duck could so ennoble a plate of rice.

Rice!—the blank canvas for chefs. Into it they may plunge whatever inspires their noses and palates. No chef worthy of his toque places before us exactly the same risotto twice—no, we never step into the same stream twice. Nor can he repeat a risotto even if he wants to, since the flavors and ingredients change with the seasons, and the body changes, and we are not the same person we were even a month ago. Nor can he truly copy another chef's risotto. But who would want to when rice allows him to shine, create, and mix his favorite flavors in their most secret shadings.

Whatever other wiles a chef has, his risotto variations remain his most fully realized hidden passion. Anyone can bake a squab. Well, pretty much anyone. But a risotto of undercooked baby clams enriched with clam juice long-simmered in far more delicate seafood stock and seasoned with a dash of white wine may well strike the palate with the outcry of a lost virginity's little death, no matter how many times we've had baby clam risotto. I'd thought of posting here a small piece about sex and food ("her tongue was peaches and dreams") but that's already been done in Tom Jones with apples and drooling pears. I scoff at ripe fruits when a great double-bed of risotto rises to my nose from the arms of a wise old wife who knows all my hungers and can drive mere squab-and-chicken sex out of the universe.

I was led into my risotto obsession but a few years past, by the thrilling Madeleine Moontree in her apartment overlooking the Hudson, along the Spuyten Duyvil coast of great chefs. Just as chefs cook quite simply when home alone (a ground meat patty with a dash of A-1 Sauce worked in), Manhattan chefs live quite simply away from the city's police and fire sirens. Madeleine Moontree even foregoes television, parking her set in the closet. The evening dusk flows from horizon to far horizon as she sets before me a long flat bowl filled with colored rice and a strange mix of saucy smells.

What's this! I ask.

Seafood risotto, she says. Each color is a different seafood.

It always comes in colors?

This is the flag of Italy. The rice is short-grained Arborio.

I see. Not Uncle Ben's minute rice?

This has taken me all day. Dive in.

Ahh! I moan. Seafood and porcini mushrooms! Shrimp! Scallops al dente! Topped with Parmigiano-Reggiano. Sumptuous—and yet so earthy. You must give me the recipe.

There isn't any. I never repeat myself.

You mean I'll never have this dish again? Not for the rest of my life!

Not until you get to heaven, Donald. But maybe I can improve on it. I have a lobster and wild mushroom risotto I'm dreaming up. But it's a trifle pricey, takes two lobsters. Cut up, of course. A little truffle essence to lend the lobster a smoky boost. And always a sweep of parmesan.

That night I go home and dream of the savory Queen of Heaven Madeleine Moontree as we fall into each other's arms and roll about in a tub of lobster risotto borne aloft during the St. Anthony's Day parade in Little Italy, a scene beloved by viewers of Godfather II. Such dreams, often shading into dementia, are the cryptic, indeed tragic symptoms of twilight and senility in aging food writers who eat too much dessert cheese before bed and then must face nightmares of public nudity or of madmen thickening their risotto sauces with flour and garnishing their table with cole slaw slathered with Russian dressing for zest.

And so it was that I entered the world of risotto and ever since have known at once what I will order at whatever posh digs I am invited to. I need but glance at the menu to assure myself that some splendid adventure lies before me this evening if I but ignore the standard entrées and follow the treasure map that Chef has drawn just for me, the thick rich parmesan and puréed artichoke risotto (God, it's almost a green cheese pudding but enriched with nutty artichoke), the simple butternut squash and minced shallots risotto, the fennel and onion risotto with peas and pecorino Romano, the red wine risotto with grated Romano and herb-crusted salmon, the even simpler shrimp and pea risotto with parmesan, the ritzy beetroot risotto, the wild mushroom and spinach risotto, the red kidney bean with fresh sage risotto, a basic chicken livers risotto, the meat sauce Bolognese risotto, the vegetarian asparagus and zucchini risotto with pine nuts, and even the Queen of Heaven Madeleine Moontree's Lobster and Wild Mushroom risotto with two whole lobsters cooked and cut into bite size pieces. (Serves one.)

She Likes My Hair
by Evan Morgan Williams

"Big sister, are you awake?"
    "No."
    "Yes you are."
"Listen, I have an exam tomorrow. Go back to sleep."
"I can't sleep. I can't sleep, and I'm cold."
"Lie against me. And shut up, will you?"
"What's your exam about?"
"Hush."
"Just tell me. I'll quiz you."
"It's on Rumi."
"Who?"
"Never mind. Go to sleep."
"Hey."
"What?"
"Do you think your roommate can hear us?"
"She's asleep. She's not listening. I'm not listening either."
"Where's she from, again?"
"India."
"That's right. She's so pretty."
"Listen, will you lie back down and go to sleep?"
"I like her hair."
"You know, when you were little, you never slept. You were always awake and complaining of cold."

"I don't remember that."
"I used to wrap my arms around you like this."
"Actually, I don't sleep at all anymore."
"That's swell. I have an exam tomorrow."
"I just kind of wait."
"What do you mean, wait?"
"I don't know."
"Yes you do. Tell me."

ꙮ

"Mom didn't want me to come visit you."
"What?"
"I had to throw a fit."
"She doesn't want to lose her baby girl."
"Don't say that."
"It's true. You're all she has. Is she still drinking?"
"I am not all she has."
"Did she give you a bunch of money at the airport? Did she cry? You both cried. Let me guess, tomorrow you'll go to the bookstore and buy yourself a college sweatshirt with her money, but you'll never wear it again."
"You went away. You don't get to say those things."
"Just go to sleep."

ꙮ

"Hey, do you ever think about dad?"
"Listen to me. Will you please stop talking? And lie down. I thought you said you were cold."
"I miss him every night."
"His cooking. I don't miss that."
"I think about him when I'm waiting."
"I still don't know what you mean. Waiting."
"You do too know."
"No, tell me. But tell it like a story, so I can fall asleep again."
"Okay. Once upon a time, there was a family. There was a mom, a dad, and

two girls, who were very beautiful."

"Gag me!"

"Hush. Anyway, this family had a restaurant in the mountains, with big clay ovens in the snow. It took forever to cook anything, and the dad had to go outside and keep the fires burning through the night. One of the girls, the younger, prettier one, used to wait for him by the door. She wrapped herself in a blue blanket and sat on the floor, and the wind shook the house."

"No, the Aspen house was made of stone, and it was always warm."

"That's not right."

"You don't remember, but it was. Maybe you've also forgotten that the restaurant failed."

"I guess I knew that."

"All his restaurants were failures."

"Mom told me he cooked for two presidents. He wrote that book. He was on Iron Chef. That was something."

"Anyway, back to your story. You were waiting by the door…"

"He was not a failure!"

"Hey, don't cry. Listen, do you remember when we spent the night in one of the ovens? You were so small. Don't cry."

"I remember the snow was blue. I held your hand and we walked on top of the blue snow."

"I sneaked out, but you followed me. The door locked behind you, and we slept in an oven. The snow falling on the oven sizzled and turned to steam."

"Where were mom and dad?"

"Where do you think?"

"Do you remember when he baked a pig wrapped in grape leaves? He dug that hole and buried the pig in some hot rocks. It cooked for days. He dug it out with a pickaxe. The meat fell from the bone."

"That was good, but I got pieces of grit in my mouth. I was afraid to say anything."

"He boiled water in an Indian basket. He dropped hot rocks in the basket and the water hissed and boiled. We had tea. The tea tasted like ash."

"I didn't like that."

"I liked it okay. Everything tasted good to me."

"What about when he fried eggs on a rock in the sun?"
"Everything."

※

"Do you feel better?"
"Yeah."
"Are you going to fall asleep now?"
"I already told you—"
"You just kind of wait. Well, I'm going to sleep."
"Hold on. Put your arms around me. Like that."
"You were too small to remember, dad made us sleep with some potatoes against our bellies. They were hard as rocks, but in the morning they were soft. No one wanted to eat them."
"I thought you were going to sleep."
"Yeah, but you don't have any of it right."
"Yes I do. Just because you're older doesn't mean anything. There's a lot of stuff you don't know."

※

"What did you do with your money?"
"Mom's keeping it for me. Some kind of trust fund."
"You'll never see that again."
"Don't say that."
"It's true. She moved you to Paris."
"But it's fun. We speak French. There's the American School. It's a good school, and it's fun."
"How do you think she's paying for that?"
"Well, what did you do with your money?"
"How do you think I got here?"
"Hey, you promised you'd take me to a party."
"It's the night before finals. There are no parties. People are asleep."
"Tomorrow night, then. We should go to a party. An off-campus party."
"You're only sixteen."

"I don't look sixteen."
"You don't understand."

❧

"Okay, this is the last time I'm going to bug you."
"Right."
"You know when we moved to San Francisco?"
"Yeah. Mom and dad were always fighting."
"No, they weren't."
"At night. You were asleep."
"Actually—"
"They fought all the time. How do you think they felt, taking those jobs? They were basically servants."
"They were chefs. We had our own house."
"On an estate! I didn't see you playing croquet. I didn't see you riding a pony."
"Our house was cool. Set into the hill. It was like in *The Hobbit*. I thought it was special, and I liked it."
"You liked the dirt floors? You liked water dripping down the walls? You liked sleeping on moss? You liked listening to those ovens? They sounded like breathing."
"Here's something you don't know: in the morning, dad and I would go into the forest with a shovel and a wheelbarrow, and come back with roots and turnips and carrots and beets and mushrooms. You were asleep."
"Actually, mom and I were in the kitchen, feeding fires, soaking clay pots, starting bread. I had to sweep the floors."
"Sometimes we took the wheelbarrow down to the creek and picked rocks. He said different rocks had different flavors. On the way back he went slow, and I ran ahead and picked roots and carried them in my skirt."
"Our skin smelled like dirt."
"You didn't like that smell?"
"Why do you think mom took us away?"
"Don't talk about that. Just talk about the good things."
"Mom taught me to cook all her desserts. We smoked cigarettes in the pantry and cooked desserts."

"Here's something else I remember: dad would set down the wheelbarrow and chase me and catch me and spin me around and around."

"Everyone did that. Mom did that. I used to do that too."

◈

"Actually, that's when I started having trouble sleeping."

"What?"

"In the motel. I couldn't stop thinking about him."

"He didn't even notice when we left."

"That's not true."

"You know it's true. He was digging up another pig. It's very tricky. It dangles from a crane and you can't leave it for a second."

"It was so quiet in that motel."

"I had a TV in my room."

"Just think, he was slicing the pig open, scooping out the hazelnut stuffing, setting it on the table, and for no one. Maybe that's when he missed us, when he listened and all he heard was the hum of the ovens. I missed him so much. I slept in bed with mom, and she had her arm around me and wouldn't let me go, and it was cold. I've never slept much after that."

"I bet she was drunk. He was probably drunk too."

"You would have let me in, right? If she had let me go, you would have let me in."

"I don't know."

◈

"Do you remember the feast?"

"I'm going to fail my test tomorrow."

"The big feast?"

"Every night was a feast."

"Don't you remember?"

"Excuse me for not realizing that a roast pig and twelve mincemeat pies and fifty pounds of potatoes and a dozen clay pots popping open every night was not a feast. Which big feast are you talking about?"

"When we were all invited to the main house. Mommy bought us yellow silk dresses."

"Oh, that feast."

"All you remember are the clothes?"

"That was the most beautiful dress I ever had. The stiff silk rustled. Mom and dad probably felt guilty about the whole motel thing. I got earrings too, and mom took me to a salon."

"But you don't remember the feast itself. See, I do remember stuff that you don't."

"I wanted to sneak out and smoke a cigarette."

"Momma took your picture in that dress. We still keep that photo. It's sexy."

"So tell me about this feast."

"The food cooked in the ground for a week. During the wait we picked roots and dad made a liqueur out of them. You and mom made all those pies. A hundred people, at least. All the big names were coming."

"I remember people were upset with him. Grit on their teeth."

"So you do remember!"

"No one wants to eat grit."

"It was part of the flavor."

"You can't expect people to eat food with dirt in it."

"Just because it was cooked in the ground! It was clean. I ate mine. I had seconds."

"The part I remember is when mom and dad threw it away. Into the furnace. The racks of pork went in. The pies went in. Whole dishes and platters went in too. Then the black greasy smoke clogged the chimneys and billowed into the house and ruined everything. That's why we never wore those dresses again. Mom and dad really had it out that night."

"She was being unfair."

"They both were ridiculous. They broke everything in the kitchen. They didn't care. Not really. That's when I knew I wanted out."

"I hid in my bed. I pulled up the covers and hid in my cold bed. I guess I was used to it. I wasn't sleeping much by then anyway. Now do you see what I mean about waiting?"

"I wanted out, and I got out."

"Hey! What are you doing?"

"I want a cigarette."

"Doesn't your roommate mind?"

"I open the window and smoke on the balcony."

"Omigod, it's freezing out here."

"Come on. Bring the blanket."

"It's cold."

"You want a smoke? You're the one who doesn't sleep. Sit next to me."

"Sometimes mom and I smoke in the middle of the night. She brushes my hair and we smoke. I don't like it that much."

"Hey, this is just like back in Ketchum. Remember when we used to sneak onto the deck and smoke? It was so beautiful. All those stars."

"It was cold. I only went out there to keep an eye on you. I thought you were going to run away. Then you moved to that old cabin up in the canyon. I missed you."

"It was a sheep station."

"You probably slept like a log every night."

"I mostly read."

"And smoked."

"Mom and dad were glad to let me go by then."

"We brought you a load of brick to build a stove. I rode in the middle between mom and dad. No one talked, but what would you talk about when your kid leaves and you're, like, helping her? Mom cried on the way back."

"I kept a fire going for eleven weeks in that stove. The bricks were always hot in the morning. You put in newspaper and kindling and poof!"

"I was lonely without you."

"Sorry about that. What did I miss?"

"I don't wanna talk about that."

"Come on. I'll listen."

"After you were gone, I saw dad punch the bread dough. He heated rocks until they exploded. That sort of thing. The new restaurant was losing money. Mom and I were together a lot. She taught me how to make desserts. I think she wanted to be pals. She bought me clothes and she took me skiing all the time."

"Was he drinking?"

"The day I got my braces off, you know what he said to me? You look different. I'm like, 'Don't you notice anything? Look at me!'"
"Was he drinking?"
"I lay awake and waited for the place to burn down."
"Duh, it was made out of stone."
"I still waited for it."
"Was mom drinking?"
"I don't want to talk about that."
"C'mon."
"You already know. Are you done with that cigarette? I'm freezing."
"C'mon. Tell me something I don't know. I wasn't there."
"See, there's lots of stuff you don't know."
"I'll believe you. Tell me."

꽃

"Do you know what it's like to be cold? Cold and alone? You lie in bed, and your face is cold, and if you move your body an inch you feel cold patches under the blankets, and you're afraid to let anything touch you because it will be so cold. But you're alone and you want a body against you. Maybe she felt the same way."
"What are you talking about?"
"Sometimes, mom came up to bed, and I could smell her, like when someone peels an orange, you can smell it across the room. I could tell how much she'd had. She was always quiet, that's the strange part, but I could like smell her in the room. Cold rush of air when she lifted the blankets. She would slip into the bed and lie behind me and wrap her arms around me. She touched my breasts and belly and told me I was beautiful. I wanted her to be warm around me but she was cold, and her lips left damp spots on my neck, and I would start to tremble and she'd be like, 'You're so pretty, You're so pretty, Don't be afraid,' and she would turn me towards her and kiss me hard. Maybe I would fall asleep, because suddenly I was alone. She was smoking by the window, and I would go lie against her until she told me everything was alright. She was always so cold."
"How far did you guys go?"
"Don't say it like that!"
"No really."

"I don't want to tell you if you're going to say that. She didn't even remember in the morning. In fact, she'd be gone. Dad was down by the river, looking for rocks, but it was frozen, and from my window I could see him walking over the ice. The floor was so cold my feet were numb, and I would wrap in a blanket and trudge through the restaurant to the one warm place. The kitchen was always a mess. Another feast uneaten, a pile of broken clay pots, the sweet smell of cardamom. Those furnaces humming. Once I took a hot rock from the oven just to feel something. I gathered it into my blanket and curled up on the floor. And even though I was dead tired I forced myself to stay awake. I didn't want to miss the first thing that felt good and warm. A rock, round and smooth and warm, rolling in my hands, in my lap, in my blanket, round as a belly. I was afraid to sleep. Sleeping is forgetting, and I didn't want to forget anything."

"You never told me about this."

"I did too, but you don't remember. You got out and didn't look back, and that's the same as forgetting."

"I'm going to miss my exam."

⁂

"Omigod, I think she's awake. She's been listening."

"She's just having a dream. Lie back down."

"I wish I was her."

"What happened after I left for college?"

"One time he cooked a pig in the earth and forgot about it. We poked around but never did find it. Then he left a pot of chicken stock on the stove, I swear, for two months. I threw it away. He catered a funeral. A baked pig was okay at a wedding, but at a funeral it was, like, bizarre, you know, digging up your meal. He was lifting the pig from the hot rocks, and it broke from the crane. The meat fell back into the fire. Black, oily smoke, like in San Francisco. He stopped working after that. You should have visited more often."

"I came back for the Yellowstone trip. That's good for something."

"You only stayed for a day. It's not like we were a family. Dad got arrested."

"At the geysers. What did he say, again?"

"'This is my kitchen!'"

"Mom took us to the lodge. We ate hamburgers and hot dogs and sodapop."

"He wanted to barbecue an elk."
"Mom bought us junk food!"
"I was glad to see you. And then you were gone."

~

"So, did you feel the earthquake?"
"It's almost light out. What about your exam?"
"Tell me about the earthquake."
"I like it when you stroke my hair."
"Tell me."
"Mom and I were in the car. We were coming back from Sun Valley. We didn't feel anything."
"I wish I had been there. I never got a chance to patch things up."
"The strange thing was, when we got to the house we could still smell food cooking. For days. We called his name and in that tumble of stones we picked around for dishes, clothes, my diaries, photos, and we could smell baked bread and rosemary. The stones were warm, and steam was seeping out, and it smelled like all the good things he ever cooked in the earth. I know he wanted it that way."
"Geez, your face is cold."
"Your fingers smell like cigarettes."

~

"Look at her. She's opening her eyes. She's so pretty."
"God, I am so screwed."
"What time does the dining hall open?"
"Five."
"Then I'm getting up with her. Omigod, your floor is freezing! You guys should get a rug."
"We don't need a rug."
"I have money. I'll buy you a little rug."
"Don't buy us a fucking rug. Listen, why don't you apply to come here next year?"
"Mom wants me to stay. She can't speak French. She wants to write a cookbook and she can't even speak French. I have to buy her cigarettes. Hey, where's my brush?"

"You should move out here."

"Be honest about something. You walked away from your life. Why? You hurt mom and dad, and you hurt me."

"This is hard to talk about."

"I told you something hard, you tell me something. Then I'll go and you can sleep in. I'm taking your blue sweater, by the way."

"Well, this is before you were born. When I was four or five I got into the kitchen. I wasn't supposed to, but I did. I remember the great stone floor, blanketed with grit. Everything warm. I remember a low noise, like breathing. It must have been the ovens. I was totally alone. Dang, where was anybody?"

"I remember when that happened."

"You weren't even born yet."

"I have to tell you something. You have it all wrong. This story happened to me. It was at night, and the kitchen was shut down."

"No it wasn't. There were kettles going and there was warmth in the floor from the fires. I saw a pile of stones and I picked one up, and I remember so clearly how it burned, and when I dropped it it broke in two and the inside glowed red, and I screamed but no one came. I screamed."

"I know it was me in that story. I held onto the stone and when I screamed everyone came. You came. Mommy and Daddy came. I knew all of you would come. I held onto the stone because I just knew."

"No one heard me. I learned to manage pain alone. You'd better go, by the way. My roommate's waiting for you."

"I just knew."

Chutney
by Elizabeth Weir

> *First paint a cage with an open door*
> —Jacques Prevert, "How to Paint the Portrait of a Bird"

Chop and dice three pounds of firm green tomatoes,
six apples and one large yellow onion. Ladle in

two cups of cider vinegar for sharpness,
two cups of brown sugar for sweetness,

three teaspoons of mixed spices for zeal. Add
four crushed garlic cloves and half a cup

of fresh-grated root ginger to make it kick.
Shake in whole coriander seeds to entice the tongue

with hints of citron, the dust and silks of India.
Set the pot to simmer for one hour. Never forget

the raisins, handfuls of golden raisins, sweet and tart,
filled with sun and rain. Stir at intervals. Boil

jars and lids separately. On a whim, toss in
slivered almonds. Taste a lick and if it fills

your head with autumn, the argy-bargy of brothers
romping upstairs and your mother's raised voice,

spoon it, two scoops per jar and screw
the lids on tight. Sponge down each

with hot water to clean off sticky runnels
and set aside to cool. If your kitchen

stays silent, it's a bad sign. But if the air
snaps and pops with the sounds of sealing

stick on labels, date and title "Chutney."
                Now, sign your name.

Scurvy
by Lanard W. Polis

Scurvy. The very sound of the word struck fear into our hearts. Not knowing what it really meant, we whispered it back and forth, hissing its 's,' growling its 'u,' drawing out the 'v' as though it were an evil hex; afraid to speak it too loudly that we might bring its curse down upon our heads.

I can't remember if there ever was any real discussion with my mom as to what scurvy actually was, or what its symptoms entailed. My little brother Peter and I knew only that if we didn't eat what she told us to, we'd succumb. And woe to any child who contracted the deadly, incurable illness, guaranteed to lead to a lifetime of unspeakable suffering—and that's if you were lucky.

"Do you know who the hunchback of Notre Dame is?" Mom would ask. That simple question filled our impressionable minds with the image of a wretched, tortured monster living out a miserable existence alone in a bell tower, an obvious victim of the Big S.

The first time I heard of scurvy was in 1962, when our family had just moved to Bethel, Connecticut. Maybe it was our respective ages, five and seven—just when the protective antibodies passed on to us by our mother had begun to loosen their inoculating grip; or was it the disease itself that lay dormant in Bethel's stony soil, waiting to infect unsuspecting children like us?

Peter and I would return from an afternoon of play, eager to tear apart the flesh of animals that Mom had prepared for us, steaks, chicken legs, hot dogs and hamburgers…But instead on mom's stovetop sat silver pots of various sizes, with bright copper bottoms, arrayed like the apparatus in an alchemist's laboratory, bubbling away with mom's home-brewed anti-scurvy vaccine. Carrots, peas, lima beans, string beans, spinach, cauliflower, broccoli, and the dreaded, smelly-urine producing asparagus, all boiled and steamed to death in those fat, ruddy-bottomed pots. Like the worst viruses, scurvy was a tricky disease that could mutate on a dime and required just the right combination of vegetables to fend off its virulent effects.

And so, once she'd boiled them to just the right slimy consistency, in her white lab coat of an apron the Dr. Jonas Salk of 6 Keeler Street would heap the recommended dosage—about a quarter ton—onto our plates. Then she'd stand there watching us eat every last mucilaginous, seaweed-like scrap. Another triumph of botanical science over pestilence.

Peter and I would sit at the kitchen's colonial trestle table, snuggled up tight in ladder back chairs, contorting our faces in disgust as we'd stare at the stinking mounds which, in our opinion, took up an inordinate amount of space on our plates, space that might have held, for instance, a thick, ketchup-laden slab of mom's delicious meat loaf, or an extra serving of corned beef, or a slice of her chocolate cake.

Alas, no seconds or desserts were to be had until mom's vegetable edicts were obeyed to the letter. Pushing the despised veggies around on our plates with various utensils under the pretense of "cooling" them was a pointless ploy, soon abandoned. There was (we learned soon enough) no statute of limitations on vegetables, and string beans tasted even worse cold than hot. Hiding vegetables in other less important foods—in the starchy folds of mashed potatoes or buried under the tuna casserole—was no more successful.

Peter and I did, however, find that with practice it was possible to swallow a wide variety of detestable vegetables without actually tasting them. The drawback to this Houdini-esque trick was the frequent gagging and occasional puking it inspired, which did little to endear us to our already beleaguered mother.

Our only real hope was the family dog, a Brittany spaniel named Beau. Beau's hunting instincts were nothing to write home about, but his begging skills were superb. And though Beau eventually passed on to his final reward, I can say with confidence that scurvy was no factor in his demise.

Mom would tolerate our charades just long enough for us to see their futility, knowing that a single mention of the "S-word" was all it would take to bring us back in line. Frozen with fear, Peter's eyes would grow as big as the plate of broccoli set down in front of him, and we would scan each other's faces for signs of disease. Back in those days, I felt genuine concern for my younger brother's life. He was smaller and weaker than I. My hair was dark and wavy, while Peter's was fair, short and straight. This, added to his stunted growth, was, I concluded, proof that scurvy had taken root and that he was soon to face a lonely exile in some godforsaken bell tower. Being the virtuous and saintly older brother that I was, I was determined to rescue Peter from this fate, willing to risk life and limb by giving him my vegetable portion. For my trouble a second helping of boiled okra was heaped upon my plate.

So much for heroic self-sacrifice.

My grandmother also knew a thing or two about scurvy, and could debate its mythical origins. One evening on my grandparent's front porch in the little land-locked town of Vista, I was doing my best to refute my mother's nutritional dogmas. "But Gram, where is it written?" I asked, thinking I had her stumped, only to be dazzled by a whirlwind historical survey of scurvy, starting with its first diagnosis in Mesopotamia, the ancient cradle of civilization. Papyrus scrolls being expensive, writing wasn't as commonplace then as it is today, Gram explained. Thus Hammurabi's Law was passed down orally, as were other discoveries and traditions. Many years later, when Moses led the exodus out of Egypt, the nomadic Hebrews were well acquainted with scurvy. Gram stressed that God had provided for them with "manna from above," a form of heavenly vegetable—which made perfect sense to me, recalling from religious lessons how the nomads were quickly dissatisfied with this "manna's" taste. I imagined young Hebrew children gathered around the cooking fires, watching with long faces the manna-vegetables being boiled to slime in clay pots.

Gram also stated that even in our time it was rumored that in Jefferson's first draft of the Constitution, our mother's immutable vegetable-eating law had been included, but a British spy among its framers managed to scratch out those fateful lines before its text could reach print in our schoolbooks. One had only to read of General Washington's near disaster at Valley Forge to see how close we came to losing the Revolutionary War. And all because our soldiers lacked enough string beans to see them through that difficult winter.

Before she rested her case, Gram submitted one final piece of evidence. She asked if I had seen any trace of scurvy in the pictures of my father that were scattered throughout the house. No I thought, he was healthy as a horse. If there ever was a guy that lived totally scurvy-free, it was my dad.

"And how do you suppose he got that way?" Gram asked. Even stunted Peter knew the answer to that one. "Here's a hint: your father was in the navy," Gram said, leaving me to ponder. What had vegetables to do with the navy? Since when did Brussels sprouts flourish at sea?

If you ever want to know anything about the United States Navy, ask one of my male relatives. My grandfather on my mother's side had been a navy cook in WWII. He served aboard a frigate in the Battle of the Coral Sea, and told us kids thrilling stories of huge ships locked in a death struggle with Japanese Kamikazes. We envisioned a sinewy, steely-eyed Grandpa below decks in the vessel's cramped, sweltering galley, dodging 30 caliber machine-gun rounds while heroically boiling huge kettles of spinach and collard greens to save his crewmates from enemy scurvy attacks. (According to gramps, the key to preparing these exquisite naval cuisines was a copious use of salt and pepper, and gobs of butter. With those three ingredients alone, my grandfather could stew seaweed and make it edible.)

From my father, who served with the Sea Bees, we got a unique nautical perspective on scurvy's history. Dad had been to some of the world's most exotic ports of call: Korea, Japan, Alaska, and the Philippines—veritable hotbeds of scurvy. Seafaring pursuits and scurvy were inescapably intertwined and even the earliest documented voyages were plagued with the disease. Dad's stories were filled with adventurous sailors on majestic wooden ships, sailing in search of treasure, only to find calamity on the high seas as their stores of fresh vegetables ran out in the windless middle latitudes. We imagined ancient mariners, gaunt and wild-eyed, suffering from dementia, brought upon them by the onset of the ailment. To these poor souls, dad would tell us, lima beans were more precious than gold.

But even I couldn't escape that decade without a scurvy close encounter. One morning at the start of seventh grade I woke up with red blotches all over my upper body. All those years of creatively ditching my vegetables had finally caught up with me and I would soon begin a new life as a loathsome, banished leper. My worried mother sought counsel from our next door neighbor, Mrs. Martin, a registered nurse. Even at my tender age I knew how the medical hierarchy worked: first came the nurse, then old Doc Trimpert, then a mortician to tidy up your earthly remains, then God—or Beeazlebub, depending on your current religious status. Thankfully, my fears were for naught. Nurse Martin's expert diagnosis: German measles, a rare childhood disorder (actually a quite common infection—but it seemed rare to me) easily rectified with just the right combination of bathtub starch and boiled vegetables. Having dodged that bullet, French-cut string beans never tasted so good!

It has been well over a quarter of a century since any of us has lived in Bethel or in fear of scurvy. And yet this disease which I ultimately dismissed as an old wives' tale turned out to be real. Upon hearing my story, our amused family doctor explained that it's a disease that's caused by a lack of ascorbic acid, a vitamin deficiency easily avoided by eating fresh fruits and, yes, vegetables. And once upon a time it was prevalent among sailors. Had our mother truly saved our lives? My brother and I are now into our forties. And though we suffer from other maladies, we are scurvy-free.

Like me, my parents now live in Florida, and my own children have had the fortune of spending many a summer vacation in their company. I imagine them snuggled up tight to my parents' kitchen table, trying to fool my shrewd mother into thinking the scarcely-nibbled turnip greens on their plates can subjectively pass for crumbs, or telling my father of the nutritional value inherent in chocolate cake, only to be met by that wry smile I know only too well (if it's not written in the Navy Bluejacket Manual, dad's not buying it).

Two truths I'm sure of in this life—absolute and immutable. My mom will not let any grandchildren in her charge perish from scurvy.

And you can't con old navy guys.

Tomorrow's Butter:
a Monologue
by GERALD BUSBY

The first time I met Virgil Thomson it was over a meal I cooked for him at a friend's apartment. My friend was a young composer who was trying to impress Virgil, and he knew a lot more about Virgil's music and music criticism than I did. I was just the cook, and I was making my living at the time selling college textbooks for Oxford University Press. As it turned out, the only thing Virgil liked that evening was my cooking, which didn't sit well with my friend. When I served the dessert, a hot reduction of fresh strawberries, orange juice with its zest, and a little Cointreau—all poured over vanilla ice cream—Virgil took one bite, then looked me in the eye and said, "This isn't kiddie stuff."

I was elated, but I didn't realize at the time just how much of a compliment he had paid me. Virgil's palate had been shaped by two distinct sources—his mother's cooking which represented the best of middle-class Kansas City society in the late 19th century, and the predominantly bourgeois cooking of Paris in the early 20th century. Virgil went to Paris to study musical composition with Nadia Boulanger. He made friends with Gertrude Stein and Alice B. Toklas, which turned out to be fortuitous. Gertrude's influence on Virgil was conspicuous in his cooking as well as in his music—bold, spare, and penetrating.

That was how Virgil cooked, how he wrote music, and how he wrote music criticism, of which he was an acknowledged master. He started with the simplest ingredients and proceeded to combine them in the simplest ways. Near the beginning of our relationship, my apprenticeship I should say—there was really no other way of relating to Virgil—he told me something I never forgot. When I asked him if he'd listen to some of my music—I had written only a few compositions at that point in my life—he said, "No, I don't want to hear any of your music until I've tasted more of your cooking to see if you can put things together and turn them into something else."

Virgil liked to operate in that ethereal region that bridges knowledge and instinct, particularly with regard to cooking and music. We, his protégées, had to possess two qualities to merit his attention—talent and a practical skill, something useful to him in everyday life. I had musical talent and instincts for cooking, so he took me on. I can hear his nasal voice now calling me on the house phone at the Chelsea Hotel, "Can you run up a crème brûlée for tonight? Philip Johnson and his sister are coming to dinner."

"Sure," I would always respond. Saying no to Virgil was out of the question, which leads me to the nature of his pedagogy. Virgil taught by example, rather Zen-like I thought at the time. When about to be interviewed by a reporter from CBS's *60 Minutes*, Virgil stated flatly that he would answer no questions that began with the word "why." "Slaves ask why," Virgil quipped, "Masters ask how." Being definitive was a practical matter, the point at which knowledge and instinct converge. It showed who and what you really were, the moment of truth.

For Virgil there were three categories of cooking—food he prepared for himself; food prepared for him (sometimes his recipes, sometimes mine or those of Maurice Grosser, his longtime companion); and finally food for company (always Virgil's recipes). I participated in the second category about once a week. Virgil liked and expected to be invited every Saturday night for chicken rubbed inside and out with crushed garlic and olive oil, liberally sprinkled with fresh ground pepper, and roasted in a hot oven (500 degrees) on a bed of rock salt. That was often accompanied by braised celery and what Virgil called "hot buttered rice." Bibb lettuce with a vinaigrette dressing usually followed with an aged *asiago* cheese. Virgil's favorite dessert was a concoction that I had first done as a cook at Ruskay's on Columbus Avenue in the 70's. It was coffee ice cream topped with a hot reduction of apricots, brown sugar, and a touch of Tia Maria. Whipped cream usually capped it off. It was wonderfully indulgent.

When he ate alone, Virgil wouldn't hesitate to open a small can of peas, put them in a sauce pan with some pearl onions (also from a can), and place lettuce leaves on top to catch the steam and wilt. He also kept canned Boston brown bread in his cupboard "Very Sunday night," he would say. "Goes good with scrambled eggs." Once when I offered to make an omelet for him and me, he reached up on a shelf of his cupboard and brought down a tiny can of black truffles somebody had given him. But when he saw me put a dash of heavy cream in the egg mixture, he quickly returned the can to its shelf. "Milk absorbs flavor; it's a waste."

Efficiency ruled in Virgil's kitchen, and nothing reflected that more than his recipes for company, the third category and the one in which I participated as sous-chef. The principal was simple—the dish must look and taste elegant and require minimum preparation.

The best example was his *coq au vin*, which he said you should make with your best Burgundy. There was an element of snobbery implied in that phrase—as though we all had a bottle of *Romanee Conti* lying around waiting for the right guest and the right chicken to come along. Indeed, when Virgil received fancy wines as a present, usually red and French, he carefully put them away on a shelf above his refrigerator in one of the two linen closets he had converted into a kitchen.

His recipe for *coq au vin* went like this: have your butcher cut the chicken in eighths. In a heavy stew pot over high heat render a fist-size piece of beef suet. Dry the chicken pieces with a paper towel, salt and pepper them, and brown them in the hot fat. Remove the chicken, and pour out most of the fat. Return the chicken to the pot with a cup—yes, a cup—of chopped shallots and a cup of your best Burgundy. Bring the liquid to a boil, then reduce the heat to a simmer, placing a tight lid on the pot. Cook for 40 minutes. That's it. You serve the chicken with the rest of your best Burgundy. Elegant simplicity. Everyone oohed and aahed.

Virgil liked to talk about cooking, too, especially about the right temperatures required to produce certain results. If someone asked about a slow simmer, Virgil placed his hand near his mouth palm down, the thumb tucked under the fingers. Simultaneously he would open and close his fingers and make a soft popping sound with his lips. You could clearly imagine the surface of a sauce as the bubbles escaped the liquid—bahp…bahp, bahp…bahp. "Just that amount of heat," Virgil would say softly.

Then there was the ordeal of eating out at a restaurant with Virgil. He turned into a blatant bully, usually beginning as we sat down and bread and butter were put on the table before we even had menus in our hands. Once I remember he looked at the busboy and said loudly, "This isn't today's butter!" The stunned server was struck speechless, then shyly asked, "You want more butter?" "No," Virgil exclaimed, "It's too cold." The boy left quickly.

Virgil told me his mother used to put out "tomorrow's butter" just before she went to bed. "It needs to be room temperature to taste right." And of course butter does taste better at room temperature. Bakers on the other hand want it cold to cut into flour, and Virgil would acknowledge that. But he was adamant about soft butter on the table. And he wasn't shy about summoning the waiter when he wanted something. Those of us who were with him at the table would cringe when he'd raise his arm and shriek—"Yeh, yeh, yeh, yeh, yeh," in his most penetrating nasality.

"Please God," we'd pray under our breath, "Give us tomorrow's butter today."

Twenty-eight years after the great Chicago fire in 1871, Virgil Thomson, at the age of three, stood at his piano in his Kansas City home and improvised a musical scenario depicting the event. From there to Harvard to Paris soon after the First World War, he developed a keen eye for observation and skill for musical composition. Thomson collaborated with Gertrude Stein on two American opera masterpieces, *Four Saints in Three Acts* and *Mother of Us All*. Returning to New York soon after the Germans invaded France, he became the music critic for the *New York Herald Tribune*. His reviews could make or break a career. Virgil Thomson was the first composer to win a Pulitzer Prize for his film score for *Louisiana Story*.

Two Poems
by Robert Faguet

Eating Chinese

Can a man really eat Chinese and recite imaginative
poetry at the same time, I yelled to Joules cause his
smacking and popping subgum chicken sounds
were beginning to get on my nerves.

I reminded the man that skilled versification required
harmonious variations on a metrical theme, possibly
a spondee now and again and Joules answered by
chewing less or more or side to side and the guy held
his breath, making little runs of clicking and chawing
as well as gobbing and honking, and embellishing
the orchestration, with snapping and crunching, longer
pauses with considerable frothing, dropping of the
voice and toe tapping runs.

My God, the song of this guy's greasy gobbling, his
omnivority and happy over-gurgling, the evocative
power of midday chomping, we were running and
rolling, and for a little while in the middle of NYC
I became beside my pal a river which you know
some say is a strong brown god.

Mushrooms

I kept telling Okerney just to forget about the mushroom following him and to consider it part of his alcoholic hallucinosis, but no, oh no, once Okerney got something in his mind like that there was no reasoning with him even though he agreed the first time the morel importuned him was when he woke up drunk in the park in the middle of a *faery ring* which he wanted us to know in no way applied to him and which Joules privately doubted, otherwise why would the man's delusions involve an organism with a fruiting body?

I wasn't surprised when the spongiformic that had Okerney all up in arms didn't start inviting its friends and relatives to come along including stump growers, delicious chanterelles, stinkhorns, Slippery Jacks and Edible Boleteins, yeah and truffles, yeasts and *candida albicans* which grow under fat ladies tits and of course *monilia*, about those I will remain mum, bread molds and an army of little dicks with pink hats organizing themselves into tribes and clans like they were getting ready to form a government of their own.

I said, Okerney did it ever occur to you that the *Eumycota* are looking up to you, maybe they see you as a leader, embodying the yearnings and aspirations of a whole people, look at 'em, maybe they're a little civilization, a Babylon, a periodic migration and the guy I could tell was starting to think through what I said to decide if that could possibly be so,

that did he have before him a great preverbal
people or were they just a rabble and tangle of
mycelia and rhizomorphs and should he get his
friend, the bearded goat they called the barber
of herbivority to finish off some of these rusts
and smuts who as much as we found them
peaceful did smell at times like decaying flesh
and did have among them a couple of real killers,
like Death Cap and the Destroying Angel.

I started to wonder if Okerney yet was starting
to dream and did he see the slender stalk of
the Nile or another great river or mountain
range toward which a people coming together
as a nation would follow and Okerney came up
to me holding an Inky Cap with tenderness
and affection between him and the unusual
agaric which at maturity its gills blacken and melt
away drop by drop and can be used for ink and
Okerney I knew had decided to throw his lot
in together with the *shrooms* cause you can't
have a great people without eventually producing
a great writer and the inky must have been it.

Three Poems
by Leslie McGrath

Succotash

A screech of shuck
and each ear bared its teeth, glinting
silver as the blade drew down the cob,

weeping milk as kernels fell,
small hailstones, into a pot
aswim with heavy cream and limas.

Butter lump oozed like a yolk.
And last, a piece of salt pork
tossed in for smoky balance.

Msiquatash, the Narragansett word
for "broken pieces," became succotash,
the stew that succored us

through Indian summer evenings
when meat was scarce, milk sour,
conversation no comfort.

We spooned from that blue bowl
not just our dinner, but faith
that broken things become

something worthy if mixed together,
fussed over a little, called good.

Like Salt

I roll a thought over
like the tongue worries a lozenge:

What is the nature of my soul?

For Coleridge, the soul was immense,
    immensely deep;
Bogan saw a soul
as a kind of domino tile;
    Szymborska saw hers
"as plain as the pit of a plum."

My soul's substance
would be measured not by weight,
    not by texture,
        not by size,
but by flavor. I am all tongue,
my homunculus more grotesque
than the grotesqueries in texts—
    poet-taster.

There's a fairy tale
in which a princess is
    banished
from her father's presence
because she says she loves him
    as meat loves salt,
too humble a claim to please him.
She suffers, prevails, honors him
    with a saltless meal
and he finally understands salt's magic
    and her logic:

salt enhances, preserves;
    salt balances; salt

brings momentary union
to self and world—
    an alchemical kiss,
all I can ask for
when my night descends
and Time's great rolling tongue,
    having tasted,
pushes me into the gulf.

How to Wolf a Cook

Prepare the *mis en scene:* lower the lights
and pour from her slim-necked carafe a half glass
of something chilled, astringent. Now let
your ravening gaze travel her nether-curves
as she spoons the stew or ladles the soup
into a shallow bowl and dresses it
with thyme she's torn from the stem.
You notice her thumbprint in the biscuit
as you bite down, a bit of gristle buried
in a chunk of lamb, the potatoes
neither raw nor soft, but to the tooth.
She's in your mouth, wrestling
your tongue into an admission
of hunger—no, need—you'll speak
her words, your breath scented of her resin.
And once you've polished her off, toe to toque,
you'll wipe your trembling mouth on her red cloak.

Eating with the Dogon
by Clifford A. Wright

The crumbling, low-rise, sprawling, congested, polluted and brown capital of the poor land-locked West African nation of Mali, is Bamako. After an interminable flight I didn't care how great the music scene was in Bamako (fabulous) nor how friendly the people were (very); I just wanted to get out into the countryside and be able to breathe. Our ultimate destination was Timbuktu, but first we were headed to Dogon country, some 550 miles to the northeast. My buddy David, his friend Steven and I couldn't wait to leave, and once we did everything took on a more promising look, including our jet-lagged selves. Although it was late January, the cool season, at midday the temperature was about 95° F.

We met our guide, an engaging and fun-loving Bambara man named Youssouf Mariko, at our hotel by the langorous Niger River, nearly a half mile wide in Bamako. Mali without a guide is not recommended since the multifarious cultures of Mali are otherwise impenetrable. The Bambara are the largest ethnic group in Mali. Of the nearly thirty languages spoken Bambara and French are the lingua francas of this former French colony.

Our driver Siddiqi picked us up in the Land Cruiser. We left for a flat countryside punctuated with balazan, acacia, gum, neré, mango, shea, baobab, and other trees. Baobab, the famous tree of West Africa, are recognizable for their scraggly branches and huge gnarly trunks. There were no leaves on the baobabs this time of year. The earth was red and the little villages we passed were identical with their brown mud-brick square one-story houses. Each village rarely appeared on a map and all had crowded outdoor markets filled with colorfully dressed people.

Mali is a democracy, one of the very few in Africa, and suffered under a debilitating dictatorship from 1968 to 1991, when a student revolt lead to a government overthrow and established the present rule. Most Malians are proud of their democracy. They are also aware of its fragile nature.

We passed through dozens of little brown mud hut villages. These were all either Bozo, Bobo, or Peul villages. The Bobo have a reputation for being hard workers, the "Germans of Mali," Youssouf explained. I learned to distinguish their villages by the round mud hut granaries outside of their compounds. The Bambara and Dogon have their granaries within their compounds, with the Dogon granaries square, not round. The Dogon are one of Mali's most fascinating people. We would soon be in Dogon country.

We lunched at the *Campement Teriya*, in the dusty ramshackle town of San, a place Youssouf laughingly called "the Paris of the Bobo people." Outside of Bamako nearly all restaurants are for tourists since there is no restaurant culture in Mali, and with the per capita annual income at about $350, families don't eat out (there is, however, a great deal of cheap, tasty street food). Happily, the dish I chose, *capitaine braisé*, was not overly adulterated for Western palates. *Capitaine* is a famous firm-fleshed fish of the Niger River, served in every restaurant and prepared in dozens of ways. In this incarnation the fish had been braised in butter and peanut oil and served with rice and a tomato-based sauce with lots of onion flavor. I loved the monkfish-like texture of the *capitaine*. The sauce was rich in onions and peanuts, though I suspect some chile and spices were left out to tame it for Westerners, as the food in Mali can be quite piquant.

The road ended at the Bani river. On its banks, with its red earth, people going to the weekly market in Djenne awaited the three-car ferry (or should I say the six-cart ferry?). As we waited hoards of itinerant merchants swarmed us, many of them extraordinarily beautiful Peul girls. I don't mean pretty, I mean sassily, self-confidently, jaw-dropping gorgeous. Youssouf explained that Peul women are noted for their beauty. I'd never been anywhere where the women are so beautiful that nine out of ten could have been super-models in the States, and said so. Youssouf thought this was hyperbole, but I assured him I wasn't exaggerating.

When we arrived in Djenne—not only a UNESCO World Heritage site, but the center of a great medieval empire—our first stop was the famous Djenne mosque, the largest mud structure in the world, first built in the fourteenth century. The sign outside said "non-Muslims not allowed." That is not a restriction at most mosques, so we wondered why. The reason, when we learned it, was quite sad. Apparently a French fashion magazine had done a surreptitious photo shoot with near-naked female models in the mosque some years before. Even though I wasn't French, nor religious, this self-satisfied cultural insensitivity on the part of my fellow Westerners made me ashamed.

After circuiting the mosque we ended up in the very colorful—literally and figuratively—market fronting it. A cacophony of chatter abounded as Bambara, Bobo, Dogon, Bozo, Songhay, Solinké, Manding, Peul and Touareg people, all in their different and extraordinarily colorful national costumes, bought, sold, and mingled. The Peul men with their conical hats, long robes, selling goats, the married Peul women with their tattooed mouths and riots of color, the mysterious Touareg with their flowing cerulean robes and black headdresses, the wide-eyed Bobo children with their giggles. Snack vendors squatted before basins filled with bubbling peanut oil and deep-fried spicy bean beignets called *accra*, which we sampled, a scrumptious departure from the ubiquitous stews.

I wanted to take a surreptitious picture of these incredibly colorful women buying fish, but my flash had been left accidently on and when I clicked the shutter there was an explosion of light followed by a collective, loud ahhhhhh that arose from all the shoppers. In Mali, taking photographs without a person's permission is a grave faux pas (we'd already had an alarming incident in Bamako). Not only was I the only male around, I was the only white person. I stood there with all these piercing eyes glaring at me. Instantly, I launched into a pantomime of "who could have done that, certainly not me!" Finding my act as funny as it was unconvincing, suddenly the women burst into laughter. I laughed too, thanked them, and left them guffawing.

It was getting late and we needed to find a currency exchange—something rare in Mali. Small change is desirable since no one can change large bills. We also had to reach Bandiagara in Dogon country. At its weekly market one could find kola nuts—perfect gifts for the Dogon, who are crazy about the fruit of the kola and treat it like edible currency. Kola nuts don't grow in Mali and must be imported from the Ivory Coast, so they're expensive for the Dogon, most of whom do not even operate in a money economy.

The Dogon are mysterious people. They believe their ancestors were visited by aliens from a double star system known as Sirius, and that the world and everything in it is imbued with symbols, meaning, and spiritual forces. Their animism is founded on a complex cosmogony first revealed to a Westerner in the 1940s, when the French anthropologist Marcel Griaule, having gained the trust of the spiritual leader of the Dogon, known as the Hogon, wrote *Conversations with Ogotemmêli*.

The good road ends in Bandiagara. Bandigara is like every other town in Mali, only redder. Their market was just winding down. While we waited in the car Youssouf and Siddiqi, who is Dogon, headed off to find kola nuts. When they returned we drove to the auberge in Sangha, the Dogon village on top of the escarpment where we would spend the night before starting our trek. As we approached the huge *Falaise de Bandigara* we marveled at the 1,500-foot-high escarpment that rose up from the plain and ran two hundred kilometers long and rutilant from the setting sun. Nestled amidst meandering streams we saw verdant garden patches. The idyllic gardens, the air redolent of onions, and the Dogon farmers glancing up and waving at us provided a warm welcome. Youssouf notes that Dogon gardens often grow nothing but onions.

Our auberge made us Dogon food, starting with what was probably the best, oniony-est onion soup I've ever had. Its foundation was a deep brown and rich onion broth. I think they made the broth first, then strained it and cooked young onions—with bulbs about an inch in diameter, some finely chopped and some finely sliced—in the broth. We also had *fonio*, a grain of West Africa (*Digitaria exilis*) that is highly drought-resistant and tastes like a very fine wheat couscous but blander and whiter. In fact, *fonio* is always cooked as a couscous in a *couscoussière*, and always served with the ragout over which it steams. Our *fonio* came with braised chicken, eggplant, cabbage and carrots in a chile-spicy tomato and onion sauce. *Fonio* is a symbolic food for the Dogon since it derives from the same root as their word for menstruation.

The next morning we were joined by our Dogon guide Ouma. We left our auberge very early as we had to trek across the escarpment and then climb down to the plains 1,500 feet below. After a few hundred feet of hiking, but before our descent, we encountered two old barefoot men drawing a series of lines, circles and boxes with little sticks in the sand. At first I thought they were two old men killing time, but they were sages, fortune tellers basically, interpreting the markings left by a fox who had visited the night before, leaving his tracings across the sacred complex. The traces provided answers to questions posed to them by villagers (I almost stepped over an imaginary line marked by a piece of wood; I would never have noticed had it not been for Ouma, who warned me to mind my step). Ouma spoke Bambara, Dogon, French and a little English, and had the most invitingly warm manner. Like many Dogon men he wore a loose-fitting white smock over a white t-shirt with white pantaloons. Some—Ouma included—wore a bonnet with tassels that frankly looked silly at first, though after a while I got used to it.

The first village we encountered on our slow descent to the plains was Ireli. Ouma guided us not on a trail, but down a series of precarious rocks. As we reached Ireli he greeted everyone and they greeted him. But this was like no greeting I'd ever heard. Instead the men sang to each other, or did something like singing. The Dogon greeting is a melody of how-are-yous that can last for minutes. It starts with one person asking questions and the other answering "fine" to each of them.

It goes like this, rapidly and rhythmically:
Greeting person: *ou séo* (how are you)?
Other person: *séo* (fine).
Greeting person: *oumana séo* (how is your family)?
Other person: *séo* (fine).
Greeting person: *ounou séo* (how are the children)?
Other person: *séo* (fine).
Greeting person: *yahana go séo* (how is the wife)?
Other person: *séo* (fine).
Greeting person: *guinea séo* (how is your household)?
Other person: *séo* (fine).
One ends the exchange by saying *ohhhhhhhhh*.

Then the roles are reversed. The greeting lasts as long as it does because they ask about everything under the sun ("how is the health of your father?" "how is your second cousin twice-removed?" "how are your crops?" etc.).

David and I were so charmed by this that we started an exchange every morning among ourselves. Most Western travelers in Mali don't bother to learn any phrases, partly because there are so many languages, so when we employed this greeting as we entered every Dogon village, the locals could barely contain their enthusiastic laughter. Dogon children greeted us with "*sa va, bonbon,*" the French-expression for "How are you? Candy? or "*sa va, bic*," How are you? Bic pen for me? or "*cadeux*" present?

Dogon villages are compact. Their brown mud huts with long conical roofs create a Hobbit-like, idyllic impression. But the idyll is an illusion since, as a Westerner trekking in Dogon country, one becomes hyper-sensitive to what culturally sustainable tourism means. In interracting with us do the Dogon change their culture? Undoubtedly. And what do we wish for them? Eternal poverty so we can be amused by their rustic lives while on vacation? It's a philosophical dilemma, and I suspect the overall impact to be negative. Even a two-year-old Dogon child with bad teeth knows how to ask for candy in French. It's heartbreaking in a way. Fortunately there's a limit to tourism, for Dogon country will always remain only for the traveler willing to shit in a hole and use a teapot for a shower.

Thoroughly exhausted after hours of hiking, we arrived in Tireli, where we ate lunch. The chief of the village, Dogulu Say, a tall, regal man who also owned the little canteen that serviced trekkers—welcomed us.

Lunch was wheat couscous with chicken. The chicken was braised in a rich tomato sauce with a little onion, small potatoes, carrots, and chile. Powdered chile was on the table. Sprinkling that on top made the meal incredibly satisfying. The chickens in West Africa are tough and stringy, so they always get stewed or braised. As it is everywhere in Mali, the bread was superb. I wondered if that was because of the bread-making tradition of French colonials. Dogon bread is a slightly dense, chewy, wheat bread with perhaps a little millet flour, baked in eight by two-inch loaves. After lunch Ouma offered me a baobab drink: raw whole cow's milk with baobab powder and baobab leaf. It tasted like a warm pistachio and cut-grass milkshake.

On our way down from Tireli we stopped at the weekly market to buy some millet beer, sold by women vendors. Millet beer is called *kognnou* in Dogon, pronounced like cognac without the final 'c.' It's a famous drink in Dogon country. Millet beer is similar to a wheat beer and lighter and more refreshing than our "regular" beer. Millet and water are set over a fire to boil with dried baobab leaves (used in place of hops). The women ladled the warm beer out of huge plastic jugs. We could have gotten drunk just from the tastings.

In the market filled with both Peul and Dogon there were also some Songhay people selling deep-fried *djiminta*, an egg-shaped Songhay preparation made with millet flour, honey and peanut butter that tasted like a crumbly peanut madeleine. The Songhay live in eastern Mali and Niger. For a nickel a bowl a few vendors sold wild grape beer. It was as good as the millet beer, but odd since one doesn't associate the taste of grapes with beer.

After two more days of trekking we arrived at the village of Koundou, where we would spend the night at the *Campement d'Amitie*, quite a nice place, relatively speaking, much better than we expected. Our room had two cots with thin mattresses, a sheet, a stingy inch-thick pillow, a screen door, and no electricity, but with a communal toilet down the hall,—the first toilet in days. For Mali, I considered this total luxury. I showered under a sun-heated drum of water and changed into comfortable clothes.

We dined on the roof. The stars were out. We ate the standard chicken stewed in tomato and onion sauce, this time with a ragout of African yam. African yams are not the sweet yams known to Americans, but a blander, starchy root vegetable. (For you botanical types, this was a species of *Dioscorea*, and not *Ipomea batatis*). The ragout was flavorful and the chicken tough. But the powdered chile on the table made the whole dish spectacular. I sprinkled on heaps and gobbled away. Still, I had begun to pine for fresh green vegetables. In the markets we rarely saw more than lettuce and cabbage.

Ouma had some *tô* prepared for him and the other Dogon. He offered me some with a big smile and I ate. Wow! This was as primitive a food as I have ever eaten. *Tô* (pronounced "toe") is made with pounded millet flour stirred into boiling water until it forms a sticky, greenish and dense *polenta*. It filled a huge wooden bowl, swimming in a viscous, olive-green sea of broth, dried okra, okra leaf, the stinky ground fermented locust beans called *soumbala*, ground baobab and baobab leaves. Not bad, but too odd for me. It tasted like the mud pies I used to make, leaves and all. The heap in the bowl could have served fifty, but four Dogons scarfed it all down. After dinner, high on millet beer, we watched the Milky Way. Without any lights below the sky was crystal clear.

After a breakfast of Dogon bread and tea we left at six a.m. for Yugana, to start our hike up and over the escarpment. Youssouf had warned us that this day would be the hardest yet. Steven, already suffering from heat stroke, bowed out of the rigorous climb, while David and I scoffed at the warning, forgetting that we're both over fifty. It was indeed a grueling hike. Still, by 9:30 we were on top of the escarpement looking out over hundreds of miles. Youssouf told us that other Americans before us had remarked that the terrain looked "just like Arizona." We walked across the top of the escarpement for a half mile, then started down.

After passing through a number of Dogon villages nestled in the cliff rocks we finally reached the plain. We had been hiking for six-and-a-half hours, up and down, and now we ambled like arthritic old men. Meanwhile the elderly Dogon in their cliff villages bounded barefoot from rock to rock like mountain goats.

We stopped at Chogu, Ouma's village, to meet his uncle and his older brother, who lived in crushing poverty. We had imagined Shangra-la, but in every village children suffered from health problems, eye infections in particular, and *kwashiokor*, a disease of children raised on a high carbohydrate and low protein diet, their bellies distended. Many elders had goiter. The Dogon live with their animals in their compounds, feces and all. The compounds are filthy and thick with flies. The guides ask tourists not to give candy, pens, or money to children as it discourages them from attending school and encourages begging.

David and I were getting good at the Dogon greeting. In Chogu we initiated the exchange ourselves. The Dogon couldn't believe their ears.

We left Chogu and headed to Yendouma, where we had lunch. The effect of our long hike was visible upon us; we all had thousand-yard stares. Our lunch was couscous with tough chicken ragout and a Fanta (a popular drink in Mali).

We met up with Siddiqi and headed for Banani, where we were to stay the night. We slept on the flat roof of the *campement*. Through the night donkeys brayed, roosters crowed, and the cold wind blew loudly. It was not much of a sleep and I woke exhausted from it. We drank some tea with the deep-fried beignets they make in Dogon country, sprinkled with odd-tasting honey, as if from bees fed on millet (though there were no such bees). There were about thirty beignets piled up on the platter. The three of us ate them all.

We left Dogon country for Mopti, an active market city at the confluence of the Niger and Bani rivers, where we relaxed at a luxury hotel, which in Mali means something in the order of a Motel 6 (with pool). Mopti harbor is a teeming, bustling port right out of Joseph Conrad's *Heart of Darkness*. There were cows crossing the river, women washing clothes, some selling carrots, men baling their pirogues (the long-prowed shallow draft river boats), scrubbing their goats, hauling cotton bales, washing their cars or themselves—all in or by the river. As we entered Mopti David asked what kind of people lived in the huts we saw near the harbor. Youssouf answered, "Peul." Without missing a beat, Steven said, "So you could say this is Peul Harbor." We erupted in laughter, realizing that this could only be funny in one place at one time to one group—us, here, now.

We slept early that night. The next day we'd take a long, off-road, across-the-desert drive to Timbuktu, another adventure.

The Schumanwich
by Rebecca Schuman

I got the epiphany for this sandwich during one of my many sleepless nights. This night had the great pleasure of being sleepless as well as hunger-plagued. (Kafka was a chronic insomniac; he once joked to Felice that he spent "half the night sleepless and the other half wakeful." But I digress.) Anyway, if there's one thing you wouldn't want to know about me but I'm going to share anyway, it's that I am nearly always hungry. Except when I'm not, like right now, my belly full of the Schumanwich, Xanadu Stately Pleasure-Dome of Sandwiches I do decree.

And therefore without further ado, I share with all one of you the makings of the Schumanwich, the Private Dick Who Gets All The Chicks of Sandwiches.

Perhaps tomorrow if I fashion myself another Schumanwich I'll take a picture, but for now:

The Schumanwich

Prep Time: 1 minute (I know, excessive, but bear with me)
Cook time: 3 minues (holy crap, I know, but hang on)
Total cost of ingredients: $2 (yowza, calm down)

INGREDIENTS:

2 slices bread of non-rye variety
Ample pat butter
2 tbsp peanut butter, any kind except "low carb" or "low fat," in which case you don't deserve a Schumanwich

1/2 green apple, sliced

+ In small to medium skillet not afflicted with salmonella, melt enough butter to grill a sandwich. Place one slice of bread on melted butter and grill on low to medium heat while you cut the apple and spread the other bread slice with peanut butter.

+ Stick the apple slice on the peanut buttered bread. Slam the whole thing down on the slice currently grilling. Smush it together with a plate (or spatula if you must be all fancy). Flip the creation over and grill the other side. Don't burn it or you'll be very sad. Grilling times vary, you're not stupid.

+ When both sides are a ridiculously delicious golden brown, slide the Schumanwich onto a plate. Garnish with remaining apple. Stuff it in your gullet and thank me later.

Why I Write
by ESTHER COHEN

So I can say
My Aunt Bessie,
82 years old
and pretty fat,
had two lovers
for the last 3 years
of her life. One,
Mister Simon Harry Hirsch,
Retired labor lawyer,
Was, according to Bessie,
"imagination defying,
well worth the wait."
She attributed her excellent
Love life
To eating cantaloupes.

Contributor's Notes

Lisa Beatman was "Dorm Mom" at a Japanese women's college. She won Honorable Mention for the 2004 Miriam Lindberg International Poetry Peace Prize, and was awarded a Massachusetts Cultural Council Grant. Her work has appeared in *Lonely Planet*, *Lilith Magazine*, *Hawaii Pacific Review*, and *Pemmican*. Her book, *Ladies' Night at the Blue Hill Spa*, was published by Bear House Publishing. She lives in Boston, MA, next to a cemetery, where she finds inspiration, perspective, and ticks.

Richard M. Berlin (richardmberlin.com) is the author of *How JFK Killed My Father*, winner of the Pearl Poetry Prize, 2002. A physician and poet, his poetry appears monthly in the *Psychiatric Times*. He dreams regularly of dim sum at Maxim's Palace in Hong Kong.

Gaylord Brewer is a professor at Middle Tennessee State University, where he edits *Poems & Plays*. His most recent books of poetry are *Barbaric Mercies* (Red Hen, 2003) and *Exit Pursued by a Bear* (Cherry Grove, 2004).

Gerald Busby wrote the film score for Robert Altman's *3 Women* and the dance score for Paul Taylor's *Runes*. He's written more than one hundred concert works and his music has been performed and recorded on the EMI and INNOVA labels. With playwright Craig Lucas he wrote the opera *Orpheus in Love*. Gerald Busby lives and composes at the Chelsea Hotel in New York City.

Esther Cohen's first published piece was in her grammar school paper, an interview with Jayne Mansfield and Mickey Haggarty at Grossingers Hotel. They didn't have much to say. Her novel, *Book Doctor*, was published in 2005 by Counterpoint. Two other books are due out in spring 2006: *Occupation*, a novel about Jews and Arabs, and *Unseenamerica*, photographs and stories by nannies, janitors, migrants, and others.

Andrew Daubigny is the pseudonym of an author whose work has appeared in *Glimmer Train*, *Missouri Review*, *The Literary Review*, *Bellevue Literary Review*, *The Sun*, *Northwest Review*, *North Dakota Quarterly*, *Rattapallax*, *Salon.com*, the *Chicago Sun-Times*, and *Newsday*. His novel, *Life Goes to the Movies*, was a finalist for the James Jones First Novel Fellowship, and his story collection, *Bodies of Water*, was short-listed for the Iowa Fiction Award.

Cortney Davis' most recent poetry collection, *Leopold's Maneuvers*, won the 2003 Prairie Schooner Book Prize in Poetry. She is author of *I Knew a Woman: The Experience of the Female Body* (Random House) and co-editor of two anthologies from University of Iowa Press, *Between the Heartbeats* and *Intensive Care*. She's received an NEA Poetry Fellowship, three Connecticut Commission on the Arts Poetry Grants, and three Pushcart Prize nominations. Her poems have appeared in many reviews and are widely anthologized.

Originally from California, **Meredith Escudier** has lived and worked in France for over thirty years. A teacher and translator, she's been published in Parisian literary journals, an anthology on tea (*Steeped...in the World of Tea*) and, among other things, is forever working on a collection of essays attempting to distill the essence of ordinary French folks.

Robert Faguet lives with his wife and children in Los Angeles, California. He has published poems in a number of journals, including *Atlanta Review*, *Tulane Review*, *Amoskeag* and *California Quarterly*.

Peter Gray is the author of two books for children and magazine articles on a variety of subjects. His company, Washingtonword, provides communication services to organizations and associations. He is currently working on a book of short stories.

Paul Hostovsky's poems appear and disappear widely, with most recent sightings in *Poet Lore, Rock & Sling, Comstock Review, White Pelican Review, Mochila Review, Four Corners, ByLine*, and others. Paul works in Boston as an interpreter for the deaf.

Mark Kurlansky is the New York Times best-selling and James A. Beard Award-winning author of *Salt: A World History; Cod: A Biography of the Fish That Changed the World; The Basque History of the World; 1968: The Year that Rocked the World; Boogaloo on 2nd Avenue* and several other books.

Leslie McGrath's poems have appeared in *The Formalist, The Connecticut Review, Nimrod* and *Black Warrior Review*. Her reviews have appeared in *The Cortland Review* and *Poet Lore*. She is the winner of the 2004 Nimrod/Hardman Pablo Neruda Prize for Poetry and a Pushcart Prize nominee. She received her MFA in literature and poetry from the Bennington Writing Seminars.

Janna McMahan has won the Harriette Arnow Prize for Fiction, the Betty Gabehart Award for Fiction, the South Carolina Fiction Project, and the Piccolo Fiction Open. Her stories have appeared in *The Nantahala Review, Arts Across Kentucky, The Midday Moon, The Charleston Post & Courier* and *Limestone*. McMahan teaches creative fiction at Midlands Technical College in Columbia, SC where she lives with her husband, Mark Cotterill and their daughter, Madison.

Douglas W. Milliken is a graduate writing student at the Salt Institute for Documentary Studies, and prose editor for the *Silk Creek Review*, http://silkcreekreview.bravehost.com. He lives in Portland, Maine.

Donald Newlove's latest novel *Blindfolded Before the Firing Squad, or The Brothers Kirkmaus* will be published by Black Heron Press in 2007. He has just completed *Passion: Ardor and Desire in Great Writing*, the cap to his Handbook of the Soul series for writers and readers begun with *First Paragraphs, Painted Paragraphs* and *Invented Voices*. He is best-known for his memoir *Those Drinking Days: Myself and Other Writers*. He believes no risotto can have too much Parmigiano-Reggiano.

Ann Pelletier's poetry has appeared in *The Antioch Review, Arts & Letters, Volt*, and other publications. She has been awarded the Academy of American Poets University and College Poetry Prize and the Arts and Letters Prize for Poetry. She lives in northern California and works for Project MANA, a hunger relief agency.

David Plumb's work has been anthologized in *St. Martin's Anthology, Mondo James Dean, Would You Wear My Eyes: a Tribute to Bob Kaufman, Poet, Homeless Not Helpless*, Canterbury Press and *100 Poets Against the War*, Salt Press, Australia, 2003. Books include *Man in a Suitcase* (poetry) and T*he Music Stopped and Our Monkey's On Fire*. His novel, *The Way Harry Sees It* will be out in early 2006.

Lanard W. Polis was born and raised in Connecticut. He now lives in Panama City, Florida, where he met and married his wife Claudia in 1979. They have two fine sons, Andrew and Brian. He loves his family and worships his beautiful black Labrador, Matte. His stories center around that magical time where there were no boundaries and all possibility still existed: childhood

Alexa Raine-Wright is sixteen and has been writing since she was twelve. She plays early music on recorder and baroque flute, and enjoys dancing tango. She lives with her parents and younger brother near Ithaca, NY.

Carly Sachs holds an MFA from the New School University and a BA from Kent State University. She teaches creative writing at George Washington University. Her work has appeared or is forthcoming in *Best American Poetry 2004, goodfoot, PMS, Another Chicago Magazine, Runes Review*, inkandashes.com, notellmotel.org and on the buses of Cleveland, Ohio. Her anthology, *the why and later*, is forthcoming from deep cleveland press.

Oliver Sacks is the author of *Awakenings*, *The Man Who Mistook His Wife for a Hat*, *Uncle Tungsten*, and many other books, for which he has received numerous awards, including the Hawthornden Prize, a Polk Award, and a Guggenheim Fellowship. He is a member of the American Academy of Arts and Letters, and lives in New York City, where he is a practicing neurologist.

Mina Samuels has published pieces on international human rights, sports and business issues. Formerly a practicing lawyer in Canada, she's taught international human rights law, investigated and reported on children's rights in detention, and edited Human Rights Watch Update. Her short story "Silk Stockings" won the Symphony Space Short Story Award. She divides her time between NYC and Vermont.

Rebecca Schuman is a threat to the fabric of society. Leonard Matlin calls her "the best time you will have at the movies this year." She is registered at Crate & Barrel and Bed, Bath and Beyond. You can get much more of her than you will ever need at pankisseskafka.typepad.com.

Liz Socolow is a teaching New Yorker (currently at Rutgers) who has lived in New Jersey with sons (now grown), and in Michigan with cats. What remains are plants, friends, memories, grandchildren, one book of poems, *Laughing at Gravity: Conversations with Isaac Newton*, and, unpublished, seventeen volumes of poems, two novels, two plays, and three volumes of short stories.

Elizabeth Weir was a winner in *Second Wind's* 2004 poetry contest and Honorable Mention in the 2003 and 2005 Loft Mentor Series for poetry. She received the 1995 Robert L. Carothers Distinguished Writer award at Metropolitan State University. Her poetry has been published in *American Poetry Quarterly*, *Sidewalks*, *ArtWord Quarterly*, *Voices for the Land*, and in *Water ~ Stone*, 2004. Two poems await publication in *Out of Line*.

Evan Morgan Williams's stories have appeared in *Alaska Quarterly Review*, *Northwest Review*, *Blue Mesa Review* and numerous other journals. He teaches middle-school Language Arts in Portland, Oregon.

Clifford A. Wright's book, *A Mediterranean Feast: The Story of the Birth of the Celebrated Cuisines of the Mediterranean from the Merchants of Venice to the Barbary Corsairs*, won the 2000 James Beard Foundation/Kitchen Aid Cookbook of the Year and the Beard Award for Best Writing on Food. His most recent books are *Little Foods of the Mediterranean*, *Real Stew*, and *Mediterranean Vegetables*, all published by Harvard Common Press.

START A MOUTH-WATERING WRITING CAREER

Sign up for Craft of Food Writing with legendary food critic Alan Richman.

Whether you're an aspiring journalist or active writer, this one-of-a-kind course with award winning food writer Alan Richman will improve your skills and give you real-world insight into the food journalism business. During 6 intense nights at The French Culinary Institute, you'll get Alan's personal attention and feedback as you learn to craft food features, write crisp meal critiques, create hot editor pitches and more. You'll also get to meet visiting industry pros. So sign up, come down and dig in!

To learn more call 1.888.FCI.CHEF or visit
WWW.FRENCHCULINARY.COM/JOURNALISM

The French Culinary Institute
NEW YORK CITY
462 BROADWAY, NY NY 10013

Celebrating 25 Years in 2005

Poetry Fiction Nonfiction Translations Interviews Reviews

MAR
Mid-American Review

Looking For Submissions To Fill Our Next Quarter Century

Mid-American Review
Department of English
Bowling Green State University
Bowling Green OH 43403
www.bgsu.edu/midamericanreview

Amy's Bread

We specialize in handmade, traditional BREads.

More than bread...

We feature morning pastries, sandwiches, salads, cookies, bars, old-fashioned layer cakes and espresso beverages in our three bakery cafés.

Hell's Kitchen	672 Ninth Ave. NYC	212-977-2670
Chelsea Market	75 Ninth Ave. NYC	212-462-4338
The Village	250 Bleecker St. NYC	212-675-7802

www.amysbread.com

128 ~ ALIMENTUM

the ultimate culinary tours to Italy

**EXPERIENCE THE MAGIC OF ITALY
ON EXCLUSIVE COOKING TOURS**
with Micol Negrin, acclaimed author of
Rustico & The Italian Grill
nominated for a James Beard award in 2003

May 2006
Savoring Tuscany & Umbria

August 2006
Splendors of the Italian Riviera

September 2006
Magical Puglia

www.rusticocooking.com | 917-602-1519

Rustico cooking

All The Best Ingredients For Culinary Education

Career Training
I.C.E.'s Career Division offers accredited 6 to 11 month diploma programs in Culinary Arts, Pastry & Baking and Culinary Management. Courses are held mornings, afternoons, evenings and weekends. Job placement and financial aid are available to those who qualify. Alumni include award-winning chefs, successful restaurateurs and highly regarded food writers.

Recreational Courses
I.C.E.'s Recreational Division offers over 1,500 one to five day hands on cooking courses a year for the general public... America's largest hands on cooking class menu! Classes include French, Italian, Latin, Asian, Bread Baking, Chocolate, Wine Tastings, Walking Tours and more!

**www.iceculinary.com
212 847-0700
50 WEST 23RD STREET NY, NY 10010**

The Institute
of Culinary Education